Karma and Reincarnation

To Geoffrey, in celebration of our joint memories of past incarnations, and with gratitude for our colleagueship, mutual support and loving understanding in the present one.

Karma and Reincarnation

A comprehensive, practical and inspirational guide

Ruth White

PIATKUS

Published in the UK in 2000 by
Judy Piatkus (Publishers) Limited
5 Windmill Street
London W1P 1HF
e-mail: info@piatkus.co.uk

For the latest news and information on all our titles,
visit our website at www.piatkus.co.uk

The moral rights of the author have been asserted

A catalogue record for this book is available from the British Library

ISBN 0 7499 2039 4

Page design by Zena Flax
Edited by Carol Franklin

Set by Action Publishing Technology, Gloucester
Printed and bound in Great Britain by
Mackays of Chatham PLC

CONTENTS

ACKNOWLEDGEMENTS

As ever, I must acknowledge the groups and individuals who allow me to teach, lead or help them. They ask the right questions at the right time, so ensuring that the work continues to unfold.

I have never directly, in formal acknowledgements, thanked my discarnate guide and spiritual teacher for his presence and his wisdom and I should like to do so now.

Names and identifying details in the case studies have been changed, but I should like to thank all who gave such generous permission for their life experiences to be used in this way.

My Jack Russell dog, Jackson, is now six years old, but has once again been a warm, constant and patient companion beside me at my word-processor throughout the writing process. He attends almost all workshops, reminding everyone to stay grounded even whilst reaching for the spiritual heights.

INTRODUCTION

A PERSONAL EXPERIENCE

Although I was born in war-torn Britain, because my father
was a pacifist, who escaped prison by agreeing to do 'war
work', I spent my early years in a peaceful country environment. My parents had been made the wardens of a hostel
for evacuees in a once-gracious, requisitioned house in
Warwickshire. Italian prisoners of war worked as farm
labourers on the attached farm, supervised by my father.

As I wandered across once well-tended lawns, through
neglected shrubberies and into the fields, I was never alone.
I was accompanied by a shining being dressed in white. My
Bible picture book showed angels dressed in white robes and
I presumed this masculine presence to be my personal angel.
I felt safe when he was near and conversed freely with him.
I gradually learned that my white-robed friend was not
visible to others and began to keep my knowledge of him a
secret.

When I was nineteen years old and training to be a

teacher, I met Mary Swainson, a Jungian therapist and inner brother of the White Eagle Lodge. (In common with much esoteric practice, all initiates of the White Eagle Lodge, whether male or female, are traditionally called 'brothers'.) She helped me to understand that the being, who had now begun to communicate with me more seriously, was a discarnate guide and that I had a gift for a form of mediumship or channelling. A discarnate guide or communicator is a being who has reached another plane of consciousness and is not currently incarnate – in a physical body – on Earth as we know it.

Brought up by strictly and conventionally religious Christian parents, the concepts of pre-existence, reincarnation, karma and mediumship were unknown to me. I was very relieved though, to have a context in which to place some of my experiences. As I relaxed into these new ideas, my shining being identified himself as 'Gildas' and told me that he had spent his last incarnation as a monk in fourteenth-century France. Since then he has become part of a large group of teachers on the 'other side' who are seeking to help humanity by communicating the wider perspective of life, which they are able to see from that other dimension. He has gone through the evolutionary requirements of incarnation and will probably not choose to incarnate again. The journey of incarnation is one of evolution through experience. When a 'quota' of experience has been fulfilled and awareness attained, there is a choice about whether to reincarnate or not.

Gildas has helped me to establish my spiritual belief system, including acceptance of past lives, karma and reincarnation. One of the first serious teachings that I received from Gildas was about the way the 'jewel of truth' has many facets. Spirituality and religion often get caught up too much in dogma and 'either/or', black and white perspectives. We are gifted, as a whole, with an innate sense of what is 'of good report'. True tolerance comes from the 'and/and' position and the recognition that there are many shades of grey. This gives less security and has complacency as its danger. Yet only from here can we really enjoy the vast richness of our differences. This is the path of wholeness rather than the path of perfection. To tread it we need to cultivate a fine discernment. It leads to spiritual growth and personal empowerment.

I became a rather reluctant infants' school teacher, but when I discovered transpersonal psychology later (see Glossary), I was fascinated by the interface between the psychological and esoteric/spiritual fields. Now, as an accredited transpersonal psychotherapist, I use my spiritual experiences, where appropriate, to enhance my therapeutic work and my psychological knowledge to give firm foundation to spiritual work. I am committed to the belief that spiritual exploration *must* be accompanied by growth into self-knowledge. The perspective of other lifetimes and karma can be used to help each one of us to function more effectively in the present time. It has been my privilege to help clients to make life-changing explorations and insights.

THE SPIRITUAL SEARCH – EXPANDING OUR PERCEPTION

There is currently an upsurge of interest in comparative religions and spirituality. Many individuals are seeking a more eclectic faith, belief or practice. There is a New Age movement linked to the exploration of human potential. People who are either more, or less, consciously a part of this movement seek to understand themselves and the relationship of humanity to the Earth and creation. They practise ecology and healing. They aspire to perceive, and live in harmony with, all the subtle spiritual forces in and around us. Their belief system is open, non-dogmatic and wide-ranging. They pursue a search for personal and collective meaning in life. In the broadest sense, this quest is spiritual, drawing threads from the rich tapestries of ancient cultures, world religions, philosophy, metaphysics and psychology.

A religion is a particular system of faith and worship. The beliefs and philosophies embraced by any one religion are formally set out as a credo and become the dogma of that religion. Some items of faith, which may have a specific context and mean less when separated from it, do not easily transpose from one system to another. Yet other items of belief, which are perhaps more linked to philosophy than dogmatic practice, might be drawn upon by seekers who search, not for a religion, but for the signs, signposts and eventually the maps that chart the territories of human consciousness and being.

In the outer world today there are few unexplored, uncharted or unmapped territories. If we want to take a journey to any part of our globe it is a relatively simple matter to obtain the necessary maps and information to enable us to plan our travel and gather our equipment. The outer world is objective, its features remaining sufficiently constant for maps to be reliable. But the inner and spiritual territories which we explore, are personal and subjective. Each individual will describe inner or spiritual experiences in very particular ways, with the result that maps of consciousness only grow from a consensus of subjective individual experience. Consciousness maps help to relate exploration to theory and to guide the quest. They both produce, and draw on, concepts that inspire and enrich the mapping process. Karma, the spiritual law of cause and effect, is such a concept.

KARMA AND REINCARNATION TODAY

The furore in the press surrounding Glen Hoddle, the former England football coach, and a controversial interview, brought the word 'karma' to many people's lips. He spoke of his belief in karma, but expressed the theory around it over-simplistically. His words were also undoubtedly reported in a sensational and out of context form. The implication read from Mr Hoddle's remarks is that a belief in karma means a belief that all people who carry some extra life burden, such as the disabled or chronically sick, are being punished for sins and misdemeanours committed in a previous lifetime. Of course, lobbyists for disabled people rose up in protest at such an inference.

In the course of this book, I shall more than once refer to the fact that karma *can* be seen as the law of 'eye for eye and tooth for tooth', but shall also endeavour to show that such an interpretation is not only an over-simplification, but also a severe limitation. Karma and reincarnation give space for compassion and a deeper understanding of the process of human evolution. There needs to be no fear of a tie-in with a judgemental, punishing authority which decrees that lives of pain, physical limitation or disfigurement will be inflicted on those who fail to get things right spiritually.

Glen Hoddle's limited, almost certainly incomplete and unfortunate statement about a belief probably very dear to his heart, as also to the hearts of many, came over in such a way as to lay the trap of hierarchy. The immediate inference has to be that those of us who are not disabled have done well or 'been good', while those who are struggling with physical challenges are serving life sentences for having 'been bad' or fallen short of the mark. Since Mr Hoddle is demonstrably not disabled, he was, by implication, seen to be ranging himself with the 'goodies' and to be judging others. He paid a high price for his inopportune remarks.

The problem of pain and suffering in life, supposedly permitted by a Higher Being of Love, is one which has exercised all who are concerned with items of faith, whatever their religion may be. As we explore karma and reincarnation more deeply, it will be seen that, within its tenets, we are probably our own most severe judges in the process of evolution. Reasons for incarnating into a life of comparative suffering or physical imperfection go far beyond simplistic notions of punishment and reward.

THE SEARCH FOR MEANING

The search for meaning is inevitably a search for a positive relationship, not only with our individual inner selves and our fellow human beings, but also with the power which moves the universe. Within such a search no single, narrow angle of perception is sufficient, neither is any approach to be condemned or ignored out of hand. Truth is seen not as absolute but as a great, rich jewel having many facets. The relationship and interaction between the facets, together with the play of light and shadow upon them, gives the jewel its depth and richness. Thus different beliefs, approaches and practices can be woven together – not in order to form a new dogma, but to enable the richest possible personal spiritual life and practice, with bridges built between different approaches.

Largely because of the influence of the Christian Church on Western spiritual thought 'karma' and 'reincarnation' have become strange-sounding words to occidental ears, yet, examining its possibilities can be like shining light on to a group of the facets of that great jewel of truth. It is in this mode that this book is written – a mode I hope the reader can embrace, so that all the possibilities, which the theory of karma can add to a map of consciousness, can be openly prospected.

Note: All quotations at the beginning of chapters are taken from a poem in Sir Edwin Arnold's book *The Light of Asia* – see Bibliography.

Chapter 1
IS LIFE UNFAIR?

The Books say well, my Brothers! each man's life
The outcome of his former living is;
The bygone wrongs bring forth sorrows and woes
The bygone right breeds bliss ...

CHRISTIANITY, KARMA AND REINCARNATION • HINDUISM •
BUDDHISM • DEFINING KARMA • PERSONAL EVOLUTION AND
ETERNAL LIFE • REINCARNATION • THE WRITINGS OF JOAN
GRANT • EXERCISE 1 PRESENT LIFE REVIEW • EXERCISE 2
MOVING ON FROM HERE

CHRISTIANITY, KARMA AND REINCARNATION

Karma and reincarnation go together like the proverbial horse and carriage. Most belief systems that include karma, also presuppose reincarnation and vice versa. In world religious thought, Christianity, as practised today, is in the minority in embracing theories of eternal life, but not those of pre-existence or re-birth.

During the early years of the Christian Church, the question of reincarnation seems to have been freely debated. Some of the early Church fathers such as Justin Martyr, Origen and St Clement of Alexandria, have writings credited to them which speak of many lifetimes for one soul in evolution. A branch of the Church, which became known as Gnosticism (from the Greek for 'knowledge'), certainly believed in reincarnation. But later, Gnostics were declared to be heretics who were to be tortured and put to death for their beliefs.

In both Old and New Testaments of the Bible there are surviving references to a belief in pre-existence and re-birth. The ancient Jews believed in the periodic return of their great prophets. The closing words of the Old Testament record this prophecy: 'Behold, I will send you Elijah the prophet before the coming of the great and dreadful day of the Lord' (Malachi 4: 5). (Elijah was an earlier prophet who had already lived.)

The following quotations from the New Testament Gospel of St Matthew give us some idea of the prevalence of belief in pre-existence and reincarnation:

> When Jesus came into the coasts of Caesarea Philippi, he asked his disciples, saying, Whom do men say that I the Son of man am? And they said, Some say that thou art John the Baptist; some, Elias; and others, Jeremias, or one of the prophets.   Matthew 16: 13–14

> And as they came down from the mountain, Jesus charged them, saying, Tell the vision to no man, until the Son of man be risen again from the dead. And his disciples asked him, saying, Why then say the scribes that Elias must first come? And Jesus answered and said unto them, Elias truly shall first come, and restore all things. But I say unto you, that Elias is come already, and they knew him not, but have done unto him whatsoever they listed [desired]. Likewise shall also the Son of man suffer of them. Then the

disciples understood that he spake unto them of John
the Baptist [who had been beheaded by Herod]

Matthew 17: 9–13

Verily I say unto you, among them that are born of
women there hath not risen a greater than John the
Baptist ... And if ye will receive it, this is Elias which
was for to come. He that hath ears to hear, let him
hear.   Matthew 11: 14–15

The early Church rapidly became involved with emperors,
popes and politics. Church councils were organised to set
out the articles of faith for Christian belief. In the year
AD 553 an important Church council formally denounced
belief in the pre-existence of the soul. It seems to be at this
moment that reincarnation and karma became separate from
Christianity – though, interestingly enough, there has never
been a papal decree explicitly against reincarnation!

The story of how the development of Christian
doctrine or dogma separated itself from karma and reincarnation is complex. Joseph Head and S. L. Cranston mention
in their book, *Reincarnation in World Thought*, that there is:
'The little known but completely engrossing story of how
reincarnation became divorced from the Christian teachings,
and through what channels, hidden and open, it survived the
Dark Ages.'

In *The Imprisoned Splendour* (see Bibliography), the
British physicist, Raynor Johnson, remarks:

Some people seem curiously and almost instinctively
interested in these topics, other, frequently religious-
minded people, feel antagonistic, as though some
strange pagan faith were subtly menacing their
cherished beliefs.

He says that the average Westerner has given little thought to the ideas of karma and reincarnation. But he believes that a philosophy of life cannot ignore these ancient beliefs. They must be carefully considered, without prejudice, in order to see if they will throw light on stages of our experience which would otherwise remain a mystery. Reincarnation as a concept presents no logical difficulties to us if we put aside our emotional reaction to the idea that we possess a non-physical element which will manifest in a succession of bodies.

It was not until the middle of the nineteenth century when the way was opened for a greater tolerance of a variety of beliefs, that the idea of reincarnation resurfaced. As Christianity's grip on society weakened, interest in occult matters, spiritualism, Eastern religions, karma and reincarnation began to revive.

HINDUISM

One of the best-known Eastern traditions is that of Hinduism, from which comes a wealth of spiritual literature of ancient origin. Many of the scripts – the *Vedas*, the *Upanishads*, the *Bhagavad-Gita* – are poetic works. All are written with acceptance, or for the teaching of, reincarnation and karma.

Many people today, from East or West, would name Mahatma Gandhi as one of the greatest people within living memory. He wrote:

When disappointments stare me in the face and when I see not one ray of light . . . I turn to the *Bhagavad-Gita* . . . and I immediately begin to smile in the midst of overwhelming sorrow. My life has been full of external tragedies and if they have not left any visible and indelible effect on me, I owe it to the teaching of the *Bhagavad-Gita*.

Bhagavad-Gita takes the form of a dialogue between Krishna, the great spiritual teacher of India, and his disciple Arjuna. A short extract will give something of the flavour and of the core place of reincarnation within it:

> Krishna: Both I and thou have passed through many births! Mine are known unto me, but thou knowest not of thine ... I produce myself among creatures whenever there is a decline of virtue and an insurrection of vice and injustice in the world; and thus I incarnate from age to age for the preservation of the just, the destruction of the wicked, and the establishment of righteousness.

Hindus believe that each person possesses a single soul which will go through a never-ending series of incarnations. Hinduism teaches us that time is circular which means that every few millennia everything will recur precisely as it has done before. Put very simply, this means that everything is predetermined.

When we die, according to Hinduism, our soul remains carrying a series of impressions called *sanskars*. These are reborn when the soul reincarnates and determine the type of person we will be in the next life.

For Hindus, karma is a very important concept. They believe that whatever you do in one life will have an inevitable consequence. If you experienced bad karma you may reincarnate in difficult circumstances in order to pay off your karmic debts. If you believe you can become a better person then your next incarnation may reflect this by allow-ing you to become embodied in a more fortunate life.

BUDDHISM

Another of the spiritual paths of India is that of Buddhism. Buddhists believe that it is a collection of thoughts or 'seed' of consciousness, not a soul, which lives on after our physi-cal death and determines our next life. Each new incarnation is a result of the past one, but it is not inevitable or pre-determined. According to Buddhism, rebirth is a curse brought about by the way humans behave in their past lives. Enjoyment of 'evil' and sensory experiences speeds up the process of our physical incarnation. Buddhists seek Nirvana – the state of not being reborn – a condition in which the 'seed' of consciousness has passed beyond desire and the need for individual satisfaction.

The following comment by Edward Conze in his trans-lation of Buddhist scriptures shows how intrinsic reincarnation is to Buddhist belief:

> It is easy to see that we could not have any 'Buddhism' unless a Buddha had revealed it. We must, however, bear in mind that 'Buddha' is not the name of a person but designates a type. 'Buddha' is Sanskrit for someone who is 'fully enlightened' about the nature and meaning of life.

Many 'Buddhas' appear one after the other at suitable intervals. Buddhism is not the record of the teachings of one man who lived in Northern India about 500 BC, but the uniform result of a regular and sudden entry of spiritual reality into this world. The state of a Buddha is one of the highest possible perfection. Therefore it is self-evident to Buddhists that an enormous amount of preparation over many lives is needed to reach it.

DEFINING KARMA

Karma, then, is a Sanskrit word associated with Eastern religions and belief systems. The *Oxford English Reference Dictionary* defines it as:

> From Hinduism and Buddhism; the doctrine that the sum of a person's actions in previous states of existence controls his or her fate in future existences. The doctrine reflects the Hindu belief that life as a human is just one of a chain of successive existences by transmigration, each life's condition being a consequence of actions in a previous life.

Karmic is the adjective from karma and is also derived from Sanskrit, in which language it means both action and fate.

A nutshell definition of karma is that it is the law of cause and effect, characterised by the biblical phrase: 'As ye sow so shall ye reap'. At one level, this law is deceptively simple, but on further examination it is deep, rich and complex.

In *The Religions of Man* (see Bibliography), Professor of Philosophy, Huston Smith says:

> Karma means, roughly, the moral law of cause and effect. Science has alerted the Western world to the importance of causal relationships in the physical world. Every physical event, we are inclined to

believe, has its cause, and every cause will have its determinate effects. India extends this concept of universal causation to include man's moral and spiritual life as well.

Smith continues by explaining that a Hindu who understands this idea of karma and the completely moral universe it implies is then committed to accept complete personal responsibility for their lives. Most people are unwilling to admit this and prefer to locate the source of their difficulties outside themselves. According to what Smith tells us, the Hindus consider this simply immature.

Karma implies a lawful world and has often been interpreted as fatalism. Although Hindus may have succumbed to this interpretation, it is untrue to the doctrine itself. Karma dictates that every decision must have its fixed consequences, but that the decisions themselves are freely arrived at. That is to say, the consequences of a man's past decisions condition his present lot. Smith concludes that this means that the path of the soul as it weaves its way through innumerable human bodies is guided by its choices. He says 'We live in a world in which there is no chance or accident; the words are simply covers for ignorance.'

If karma is considered mainly as a system of punishment and reward then the life journey it reflects might be seen in categorical black and white terms. To some, the very idea of karma and many lifetimes seems symbolic of a treadmill, 'the wheel of re-birth' from which there is no escape until we are perfect. The biblical, Old Testament rendering of the law of cause and effect is: 'Life for life, eye for eye, tooth for tooth, hand for hand, foot for foot, burning for burning, wound for wound, stripe for stripe' (Exodus 21: 23).

PERSONAL EVOLUTION AND ETERNAL LIFE

Most spiritual and religious teachings embrace the idea of personal evolution and eternal life. Spiritual discipline, effort and virtue, we are told, bring heavenly rewards. Often cause and effect are seen as being immediate and sequential, with effect following cause as surely as night follows day. To some extent this is the pattern of life. The emotional and mental maturity of ourselves as individuals is often judged by the degree to which we have developed foresight and can take full responsibility for the results of our actions and interactions. Yet, if our life on Earth is limited to only one span of three score years and ten, how *do* we account for the discrepancies which are meted out to individuals as they are born?

THE PROBLEM OF SUFFERING

Existentially, the problem of human suffering, disease, disability and inequality is always with us. Taken within the context of one lifetime existence can only be seen as grossly unfair. What hand, eye, force or will determines whether we should be born male, female, black or white? Wanted, welcomed, loved, respected? Or, unwanted, unwelcomed, unloved, rejected? With or without the potential to be clever, healthy, beautiful, creative, fertile or powerful? Who, or what, determines the socio-economic scene into which we are born and which will affect the whole spectrum of our opportunity and development? Is the powerful hand of destiny random or pre-meditated? Beneficent or malicious? Do we have a positive personal destiny or is each one of us, in some way, a victim of fate? Are we self-determining or are we merely pawns, played by an almighty hand on a giant cosmic chessboard?

Many of these questions have deservedly been called 'the great imponderables of life'. Yet, as we search for meaning, we *do* ponder them and seek answers. Obviously, to some extent, the theories we arrive at and live by must be in the nature of 'working hypotheses', but this does not prevent them from bringing inspiration and motivation to life. Having a reference model can be of enormous help to living life creatively and to avoiding the pitfalls which may arise if we take the limited viewpoint and see ourselves *only* as the victims of fate.

REINCARNATION

Reincarnation, or the notion of human evolution through many lifetimes, goes hand in hand with the concept of karma and offers us a map of consciousness and being. This map will take us beyond the limited, immediate, here and now ideas of cause and effect, as well as offering illumination on some of the questions above.

In incarnation, at any given moment, we may be so close to our actions, so inexperienced, blind or prejudiced that we cannot view their effect dispassionately or objectively. When we consider the causes we have set in motion we may become overwhelmed by guilt or despair. 'If only', we say, 'I could just go back and start again, how differently I would do it now, with hindsight.' Of course, within a lifetime, as we know ourselves better and grow wiser through age and experience, we can do much to redeem past mistakes, and to integrate any learning from them. We can make regular life reviews and 'turn over a new leaf'. Wisdom often emerges from experience and our present lifetime can, indeed, be a conscious spiritual evolution.

Yet the doctrine of karma and reincarnation teaches that a system of life review and subsequent choice goes on beyond incarnation and the Earth plane. Evolution, or the spiritual perfecting of self, is given a wider context. Death is not an end, but an opportunity for a new beginning. Our consciousness continues and is eternal. Between lifetimes we review our experience, mistakes and achievements and make choices as how best to continue our evolution. When these reviews and choices have been made, and the law of cause and effect has been understood in a wider context, some new edition of that which we call self is born again, to continue the learning process. We die in order to return and each successive lifetime gives *chosen* openings for broadening experience, finding deeper meaning in life and for spiritual evolution. Instead of the 'three score years and ten' of one lifetime, there are aeons in which to discover every aspect of life and development, with numerous chances for us to correct imbalances and mistakes previously made.

The unfairness and inexactitudes of life, as seen at any given moment, continue to exist but begin to show meaning within an amplified perspective when we embrace the idea of karma. The hardships we endure, the repetitive lessons, denials or obstacles that life throws up for us take on a deeper significance. We do not have to see ourselves as the helpless, insecure victims of random selection and feel short-changed or unfairly treated by God, Goddess, Great Spirit or the Unseen Power behind the universe. Instead, we can seek to understand the choices we have made, the lessons we are learning and the causes we are redeeming. This enables us to grow in the ability to exercise a wiser, immediate control over our lives. We can see that all human beings are on a path of learning and can find and value our own place in personal and collective spiritual endeavour.

The knowledge that we have opportunities to start again or to continue our evolution on a grander scale can be comforting. If each one of us has lived many lifetimes then, excitingly, in essence, we have been present throughout the whole evolutionary journey of humanity upon the Earth. We are not transitory visitors, simply adding our lives to history but active co-creators of that history.

Many lifetimes and the karma we set in motion lead us, eventually, individually and collectively, to a full realisation of all our potential as human beings. Travelling such a journey may lead us to see wholeness, rather than moral perfection, as our goal, with karma as a law of compassion and positive opportunity.

THE WRITINGS OF JOAN GRANT

Joan Grant found herself to have a very unusual ability for 'far memory' (her phrase). She could recall a number of other lifetimes in exciting detail. In order that these accounts could be more widely read, without prejudice, she decided to produce them as novels (see Bibliography). Later, when she wrote her autobiography, *Time Out of Mind*, she described how these memories had come to her.

There is a particular emphasis on lifetimes in Egypt. Since the ancient Egyptians believed in reincarnation and karma, the books also contain teaching about these subjects.

In *Winged Pharoah*, Joan remembers herself as Sekeeta, a young girl destined to become joint Pharoah with her brother, Neyah. While Neyah trained as a warrior, Sekeeta went to the temple to train as a priestess of Anubis. In the temple, a place of wisdom where all people came for healing, practical help and spiritual guidance, Sekeeta learned seership and healing. When her father, Za-Atet died, Sekeeta and Neyah ruled their people together. The Egypt she describes at this time is a country where ethical codes relating to the dignity and value of every individual were honoured and where wise justice was available for all who needed it.

In later books, *Watchers of the Horizon* and *Eyes of Horus*, Joan describes coming back to Egypt when the country was in trouble. The temples were places of commerce and false priesthood. Pharaoh and those who governed their people were corrupt. In this time, Joan remembers reincarnating with the express purpose of forming a movement to overthrow the corrupt systems and to re-establish ethical values in law, in commerce and in the spiritual life of the people. Her experiences of high standards in her previous life informed her actions in the next. A group of those she had known and worked with before also reincarnated at that time. They came into incarnation again, gradually to make conscious in their lives, a group task of service to others and to the country they loved and remembered.

Coming back into incarnation with such a task can be seen as using karma purposefully, positively and with a redemptive task in view. In this instance, karma also goes beyond the personal and links into the group and the collective (see also Chapter 3, page 45).

In her first incarnation in Egypt, Joan (Sekeeta) benefited from what was already established. In the subsequent incarnation her personal karma involved learning to create, from scratch, the conditions she had previously enjoyed.

Using karma in this way, makes for clarity of consciousness and broadens the experience of the soul.

In Joan's more contemporary incarnation, which began in 1907, as she recovered her vivid memories of other lifetimes, she felt the need to write about her experience of times when there existed a 'fundamental and timeless code of attitudes and behaviour toward one another on which the health of the individual and society depends'. Each one of her 'far memory' novels explores a facet of this code.

In 1960 Joan married Denys Kelsey, a psychiatrist, and they discovered a way of working together to help people through severe neuroses by uncovering the roots of their trauma in other lifetime experiences (see also Chapter 4).

Embracing the theory of karma can enable us to slough off old, negative conditioning about the nature of the human journey and to broaden our vision of the power behind the universe. It encourages us to see ourselves not as banished from paradise, but on a sacred journey of knowledge, which is an integral part of the perfecting and manifesting of creation. This journey of consciousness may be painful, dangerous and full of pitfalls but it culminates in the attainment of a universal state of health, harmony and peace.

Other explorations are required as we go beyond the simplistic definition of karma as the law of cause and effect, or eye for eye and tooth for tooth. In order to deepen our understanding, we also need to examine the concept and organisation of certain other subtle worlds, which lie beyond our immediate, incarnate perceptions. What is the nature of the soul and its evolution? How are the unseen worlds organised? Within what sort of cosmology do theories of karma and reincarnation fit? The next chapter begins to explore these questions. Meanwhile, as a preparation for applying the theory of karma to your own life, try the following life review and 'moving on from here' exercises now.

Exercise 1: Present Life Review

(1) The Mental Approach

Take a piece of paper or a notebook and write down the question: 'Where am I now?'

Reflect on this question, assessing how you see yourself in life at the present time. Consider physical, mental, emotional and spiritual perspectives to the question. Get a sense of the obstacles you have faced in life, what you have done about them and the achievements you have made.

Be positive in your comments on yourself, recognising that there is no courage without fear, that endurance in itself may be an accomplishment and that few leaps are made without hesitation.

(2) The More Intuitive Approach

Take a large sheet of paper and some crayons. Centre yourself in front of your paper with your body in a balanced, symmetrical position.

Be aware of the rhythm of your breathing and gradually bring that rhythm into your heart centre or chakra, which is in the centre of your body, on a level with your physical heart (see Glossary).

Within the resulting heart breath, hold the question: 'Where am I now?' When you are ready begin to *draw* a review of your life in any way which appeals to you. Either go backwards through your life from the point where you are now, or start at your birth and work *towards* the point where you are now. You may find yourself drawing symbols, colours or an undulating line, representing the highs and lows of your life. Take time with this drawing, maybe returning to it more than once.

Compare what you have drawn with the mental thoughts and notes you recorded in response to this question.

This exercise forms a basis for later work on identifying karmic themes and tasks (see Exercise 5, page 82 and Exercise 7, page 105).

Exercise 2: Moving On From Here

(1) The Mental Approach

Take a sheet of paper or notepad and consider two questions, making notes, as you reflect:

(a) What do I want to change?

(b) How can I begin to implement this change?

(2) The More Intuitive Approach

Prepare as for (1) in Exercise 1, but have two pieces of paper ready this time.

Draw your symbolic or intuitive response to the two questions above, using a separate sheet of paper for each question, and re-centring yourself into the heart breath between each consideration. Take time over your drawings, maybe returning to them more than once.

Compare your drawings with the mental thoughts and recordings you made in response to these questions.

Over the next few days note down any life insights or emerging new perspectives these exercises may trigger. Keep your notes and drawings from these exercises for use with Exercises 5 and 7 (pages 82 and 105).

Chapter 2
THE
COSMOLOGY
OF KARMA

Ye suffer from yourselves. None else compels
None other holds you that ye live and die,
And whirl upon the wheel and hug and kiss
Its spokes of agony . . .

THE LANGUAGE OF KARMA • A WORKING MODEL •
THE MANIFESTATION OF DIVINE AND
SOUL PURPOSE • SOUL AND SPIRIT • EXERCISE 3 BUILDING
A SENSE OF THE WIDER OR GREATER SELF

THE LANGUAGE OF KARMA

We are here, on Earth. We have bodies, emotions, minds and spirits. The essence, which lies within each one of us, as an individual, is more than the sum total of body, mind, emotion and spirit. We observe and study ourselves. We debate the aforementioned 'imponderable' questions (see page 16). Thoughts about life and its spiritual implications also, almost invariably, include the questions: Why am I here? Did I exist before I was conceived and inhabited my mother's womb? Will I continue to exist when my physical body dies? A spiritual rather than a specifically religious language can help us towards deeper understanding here. Such a language may derive from different sources where, in order to explain how we came to be here, words and concepts, such as soul, spirit, destiny, free choice, higher or Divine Principles and evolution, are considered alongside others or amplified by them. In this instance, these concepts would be: incarnation, reincarnation, karma, evolution and the higher self.

The soul and spirit are everlasting, indestructible and eternal. This belief pertains to most spiritual and religious thought, irrespective of whether the central focus is on living one or many lifetimes, in order to further experience and evolution.

Destiny and free choice, also central themes in philosophical or religious thought, inspire yet more questions. Is there a set pattern to our lives? Is choice merely an illusion? Do circumstances always conspire to block certain paths while leaving others open? Is this a conspiracy managed by some universal, overseeing force? Or is destiny a matter of conscious choice? Are we completely free to regulate our lives according to whim or ideology?

Higher or Divine Principles represent the highest ideals of living and relating that we know, glimpse or imagine as individual or collective human potential. They are standards to aim for as we evolve. Lives lived and communities governed by these principles reach universally acknowledged standards of excellence and reflect hope for humanity. The fully evolved being has incorporated, understood and is able faultlessly to practise higher principles.

Incarnation means embodiment, being conceived, gestated, clothed in flesh and born. In addition to the spiritual implications there are emotional and physical factors to be considered.

Reincarnation presents the possibility that each soul may incarnate not just once, but many times in order to further the process of evolution.

Karma, the central theme of this book, is the Sanskrit word for the fascinating, spiritual law of cause and effect.

The higher self is a part of the soul, an overseeing intelligence, intent on gathering and processing the experience required to further evolution.

By setting these key words into interaction, a basic working model emerges, as follows.

A WORKING MODEL

The soul, whose wisdom and experience is gathered by the overseeing intelligence known as the higher self, is intent on evolving into wholeness or perfection.

The spirit is the pure, animating essence of being and is fully present within each one of us in every incarnation. The soul, however, remains on a different plane of consciousness, overseeing the process of evolution through the auspices of the higher self.

The goal of evolution is enlightenment, perfection or wholeness in which there is a complete at-one-ment with the higher principles. This is a state of being, beyond attachment and the limitations of the finite mind. Once this point is reached there is no longer any need to incarnate because the goal of union with the Divine Source of All Being is within reach.

The pitfalls of the learning process mean that karma, the spiritual law of cause and effect, is activated.

From karma comes the concept of reincarnation – or many lifetimes – in which to gain experience and learn the consequences of misuse or misinterpretation of the Divine Principles, as well as to learn to live from them in all interactions. In each lifetime, progressively more awareness of the need for communion with our souls and for greater understanding of individual and collective human purpose is acquired.

The higher self takes an overview before and after each incarnation in order to assess progress, make choices, open opportunities or provide specific learning situations relevant to the soul's evolution. Consequently, each incarnating being carries the seeds of destiny and many choices originate from another level, or plane, of being and consciousness.

Divine Principles are pure, abstract forces affecting and motivating us at all times. As we experience and interpret them so we name them: Love, Justice, Peace, Beauty, Purity, Harmony, Power, Service, Wholeness, Healing and Perfection. We struggle to live by these principles, but their essence defies definition. We need images, myths, symbols and personifications to help us in understanding the depth and breadth of them. As we break them down into their component parts, so archetypes are created. By dictionary definition, archetypes are 'primordial images inherited by all'. Tarot cards, which have ancient origins, have twenty-two personified or symbolised archetypes in the major arcana or suite of cards which represent the mysteries of life. These cover most aspects of human experience. (See also Chapter 3, page 53 and the Glossary.)

A consideration of archetypes can give us a fuller comprehension of our life aims, drives and blockages. In understanding the archetypes or higher principles most manifest in our lives, we can gain insight into our karmic or evolutionary life purpose. One way of looking at karma, reincarnation and evolution is to see it as a process whereby we learn about the positive and negative sides of each of the great archetypes. Can we truly know what peace is, until we have known war? Do we appreciate justice unless we have seen or experienced the effects of injustice? Can we work in true consciousness for the positive aspect without experiencing the negative? Do we know what we want without knowing what we do not want?

Higher archetypes are the pure energies emanating from the Divine Source, such as Love, Beauty and Peace. Lower or degraded archetypes derive from the higher qualities. They are often personified and arise from our struggle to understand and come to terms with archetypal forces. Thus, Love becomes The Lover; Beauty, the Maiden, Youth, Princess or Prince; Peace, The Peacemaker.

Although archetypes affect historical ages, nations, races, governments, cities, towns, groups, families, and each one of us as individuals, they can be tricky to understand. The following case history may help set this idea in context.

Case Study: John

In his early forties, John was following a successful career as a teacher. He was a well-respected departmental head in a large secondary school. To all appearances he seemed to be the epitome of the career teacher, on the brink of further promotions and success. He was happily married to Ursula, also a teacher, who had recently become head of a local village school. They had a comfortable home and their son and daughter were both doing well at university. To the onlooker, they seemed to have achieved that rounded contentment in life, which can be so elusive.

When John came to see me he outlined his basic problem as 'disillusionment and loss of direction'. He felt that his life and career had lost their meaning and even wondered if he had known real meaning in its deepest sense. He felt depressed, isolated and at a dead end. Outwardly he was trying to behave as normal but inwardly he was under considerable stress. The idea of changing his career or life direction seemed too awful to contemplate. John felt that if *he* changed the whole family would be adversely affected. Furthermore, there was nothing John passionately wanted to do instead of teaching. But, if he remained in this career, he despaired of finding the inner and outer strength to maintain the high standards he had always set for himself and which were now automatically expected of him.

I felt that John was experiencing a degree of mental and physical burnout, as well as being in a spiritual crisis, in its widest sense. We discussed measures for dealing with the burnout and I then began to talk to John about archetypes of purpose.

He felt that he had rather drifted into teaching, since at school he had not wanted to be a doctor, lawyer or priest and, at the time, teaching had seemed the only other alternative. Until recently it had fulfilled him. Now he was finding it difficult to maintain momentum but could not see any viable alternative. Somehow his relationship with the archetype of teacher had never been fully forged; he felt swept along by it; that it was in charge of his life and had cut off all other avenues. In some ways he felt he was the victim of the archetype. As he left for a holiday, to deal with his mental and physical burnout, John declared that he would take time to think about the archetype of the teacher, but also others (see page 53), to see if any energised him more.

When John returned to our sessions, deep reflection had convinced him that he had not so much drifted into teaching for lack of other choice, but that teaching had subtly called him. 'I *do* feel myself to be an educator,' he said.

Clarity about his need to go on working in the field of education made John see that he needed to find change within his profession. He was caught, not by the archetype of the teacher, but by the expectations about the pattern of his future career coming from those around him. The aspect of teaching that currently excited him most was the work he did with younger teachers, helping them to find their feet in their chosen career and supporting the development of their teaching skills and strengths. While reading teaching journals his attention had been drawn to vacancies for lecturers in teacher training. He felt he would need to do some part-time courses before applying for such a post, but becoming a trainer of teachers was now his clear goal. He felt revitalised and that his dead end in life had become a crossroads, with his feeling confident now as to which direction to take.

Karmically and evolutionarily a crisis such as John's serves to make us more fully conscious about our direction. At one level the consciousness John gained served him in being able to make a clear choice for this present lifetime. At another level, one might see that, at this stage in his evolutionary journey, he was learning to serve the archetype of teaching and the purposes of his soul for this incarnation more effectively.

THE MANIFESTATION OF DIVINE AND SOUL PURPOSE

This complex model, as so far described, implies that we have an active, reasoning, logical consciousness or intelligence, which exists before we enter our bodies in order to live on Earth and continues to exist after we die. It also implies that there are complex, highly organised worlds where existence and evolution continue. In such a model, incarnation and evolution on Earth are of great importance, but it is as though Earth is the stage where the dramas of growth may be enacted. Before taking the stage we take part in the creating of the characters and the writing of the dramas. We share in the direction of that which is to be played out.

The manifestation of Divine Purpose is very complex and beyond the capacity of the finite mind to imagine or understand. Most religions and spiritual teachings, which agree on continued existence, speak in their different ways, of higher guides, fully evolved beings, ascended ones, masters, angels, record keepers and higher or overviewing consciousnesses. These beings, existing in the more rarefied spheres, planes or states of consciousness, help and advise us on the setting of our each and every incarnational stage. They are compassionate counsellors rather than authorities, meting out punishments and rewards. In the most immediate and personal sense it is a combination of *soul, spirit* and *higher self* that oversees our evolution, and makes decisions and choices relating to its furtherance.

In order that we may be progressively schooled by life, the higher self takes an overview before and after each incarnation in order to assess progress and to draw up subsequent life plans relating to our evolution. As a result of this overview certain choices are made. In ensuing lifetimes, experience must be broadened in order to further evolution, imbalances that have occurred must be balanced and faults against the higher principles redressed.

It is for this purpose and from this point that the karmic law of cause and effect originates. To some extent the 'as you sow shall you reap' continuum will operate. If we have been unloving in one lifetime, a consequent lifetime may have an agenda for us to work hard in order to gain love. If we have been unjust, future life choices may include the experience of injustice. If we have caused strife or insurrection, we might need to be victims of these forces. If we have destroyed beauty, we might experience some sort of deprivation of beauty. If we have disrespected harmony, we might choose chaos. If we have misused power, we might choose to experience weakness. If we have failed to serve anyone or anything except ourselves, we might opt for the learning of humility. If we have been bigoted or narrow-minded, we might choose to be on the receiving end of such attitudes. If we have missed opportunities for healing ourselves or others in body, mind or spirit, we may take on the burden of living unhealed. If we have been without any vision or motivation towards growth or perfection, we might plan a life where much will be required of us.

Yet, although this level does exist, it is too simplistic. Karma uses opposites and polarities as part of its mechanisms, but encompasses far more than the reflection of evolution as a constant yo-yo process between one extreme and another.

In the retributive/repentant phase of karma (see page 56) there is an element of 'eye for eye and tooth for tooth', but karmic resolution only comes when we go beyond any concept of crime and punishment and learn to work, actively, for the higher principles. If we have created war, we may not need to be born again as a victim in a war zone. An overview of a warring life may inspire in us an understanding of peace and a passion for it, so that we choose to reincarnate as a peacemaker. Often, we only value, name or learn to work for something by also knowing its opposite. Choosing to work for the opposite of what we have naïvely or unthinkingly meted out to others makes a truer balance than merely incarnating to be persecuted while someone else becomes our persecutor. Experience of polarities or extremes can focus our attention and understanding on to what is right, comfortable or desirable, in the highest sense. Thus, some encounter with adversity may be necessary in the process of triggering awareness. Once awareness is activated, punishment, retribution or deprivation has achieved its purpose. Reaping the negatives we have sowed need not be a life sentence.

Presenting these patterns as a basis for understanding life and incarnation raises yet more questions as to the nature and organisation of the soul, its relationship to spirit and to the incarnate personality.

The model I use in my teaching, as a basis for understanding and further discussion, emerges as follows:

There is an Essence or Intelligence that conceived and created the universe, and goes on conceiving and creating it. This Essence is Divine but not anthropomorphic. All religions and spiritual teachings struggle to define this Intelligence but all recognise it. Thus, some speak of God, while others use terms such as Great Spirit, Creator, Goddess, the Divine or the Almighty. Many religions, recognising the difficulties and pitfalls of precise definition, honour the myriad aspects of creation and therefore name and mythologise numerous Gods and Goddesses. Hinduism has chants reciting the thousand names of God.

For economy, clarity and the sake of avoiding the trap of patriarchal terminology and the masculine/feminine debate, I elect to speak of Essence, the Source, the Divine, the Divine Essence or the Divine Source.

Our souls originate as sparks from the Divine Source. The original spark has a long journey of evolution ahead of it because the human choice is for consciousness, knowledge and experience, rather than for a perpetual state of innocence. Only by becoming conscious and owning our role of co-creatorship in the universe can we become truly a part of creation and *know* and activate the divine spark, which is our origin.

SOUL AND SPIRIT

The divine spark consists of soul and spirit. These two interact constantly in the process of evolution. The spirit inhabits us when we descend into matter, our souls register and assimilate all our experience. A higher self takes an overview and directs our choices. This aspect grows ever stronger as an intrinsic part of evolution.

The whole of the soul does not incarnate. One of the things that it is important to remember in a creative understanding of evolution and karma is that if we speak of past lives and say, for instance, 'I believe I was a Roman slave', it is not 'I' as I experience myself now, that was the Roman slave. The Roman slave was a separate, self-determining universe. Thus, the soul may be graphically described as the central thread of a necklace, which holds many beads, or the central core of a head of grain, which holds many grains. The beads on the thread or the grains on the core are the aspects that incarnate. When a bead or a grain returns to the thread or the core it takes back a piece of experience and knowledge, which informs the evolution of the whole necklace or whole head of grain. The thread or core stores and integrates this knowledge. When all beads or grains have returned to the thread or core the phase of evolution that includes incarnation is complete, but learning and service on other planes continues until, with the coming of Mastery or Ascension, there is a reabsorption into the Divine Source.

When we have lived many lifetimes on Earth in order to gain enough incarnate experience we have 'mastered' that phase of existence and so move on permanently to life on other planes. This moving on is often called 'Ascension'.

In this way, evolution is a composite process. The Divine Source itself is not static but is incremented by every part of the complex journey of each original spark, which was, itself, produced from that source.

The above description completes the basic model and provides most of the working vocabulary from which the further implications of karma can be explored.

In the next chapter we move on to look at the all-important issues relating to karma and choice. The following meditative exercise is intended to help you to build a sense of a wider or greater self, thus helping to integrate soul theory with your personal feeling or experience.

Exercise 3: Building a Sense of the Wider or Greater Self

This is a guided meditation that introduces the idea of an essence or eternal being, which goes beyond the present awareness of body, mind and emotions.

Make sure that you won't be disturbed. Sit or lie comfortably with your body balanced and symmetrically arranged. Be aware of the rhythm of your breathing and let it become quiet and unforced.

Become aware of your body. Feel its contact with the chair, couch or floor. Feel the texture of the clothes you are wearing, not only by touching them with your hands but also by knowing their contact with the whole of your body. Be aware of any bodily discomforts you have, any feelings of unease with your body shape or bodily functions. Acknowledge the autonomous systems of your body: blood flow, immune system, cleansing, eliminative and digestive processes, your heart beat, your breathing. Acknowledge your sexuality. Having recognised all these things, say to yourself, several times, as a mantram: 'I am more than my body'.

Become aware of your emotions. Now you may be beginning to feel peaceful, but you may have touched into some deep feelings about your body. Allow them to be. Watch them. Review your day, working backwards from this moment. What emotions have you known today? Joy? Anger? Sadness? Contentment? Jealousy? Bitterness? Grief? Irritation? Peace? Pleasure? Hatred? Love? Do not judge these emotions, just acknowledge their presence in your life and your ability to feel them. Let them pass and say to yourself, several times, as a mantram, 'I am more than my emotions'.

Become aware of your thoughts, your philosophies, your wishes and desires. Review as many of the thoughts, of which you have been aware today, as possible. Acknowledge their presence in your life. Acknowledge the power of your mind, then relax in its presence and say to yourself, several times, as a mantram, 'I am more than my thoughts, more than my mind'.

Feel light and non-attached, feel the essence of self that goes beyond body, emotions and mind. Sense its quality and perhaps its colour. Welcome it as the flame of your eternal being, let it refresh you and heal you for a while.

Before you resume your normal tasks, spend some time stretching and walking, being conscious of the contact of your feet with the ground. Draw a cloak of light, with a hood, around you, so that you carry light with you, but are also protected and contained by it.

Chapter 3
A QUESTION OF CHOICE

Before beginning, and without an end,
As space eternal and as surety sure,
Is fixed a Power divine which moves to good,
Only its laws endure . . .

THE POWER OF CHOICE • THE HIGHER PROCESS OF CHOICE •
KARMA, EVOLUTION AND THE HIGHER PRINCIPLES • ACTORS IN
THE WINGS • EVOLUTIONARY CONCERNS • KEY WORDS FOR
LIFE • RETRIBUTION, REDEMPTION AND TRANSCENDENCE •
EXERCISE 4 MEDITATIVELY OR INTUITIVELY
CONSIDERING YOUR KEY WORDS FOR THIS LIFETIME

THE POWER OF CHOICE

The law of karma, or cause and effect, becomes compassionate when we understand that our life choices are made by
our own, individual, eternal and self-determining consciousness. Our position in life, the benefits, deprivations and
obstacles we are born with or meet, are not life sentences
imposed by some judgemental being, force or body, but are
conditions taken on by our higher selves to further our
learning, evolution and experience.

One of the main tasks of evolution, and a primary
purpose in terms of karma, is to become more conscious
of ourselves and the experiences we are having, in order to

activate our power of choice. For many of us it is exactly this power that we find so formidable. How do we choose? We have to keep in mind that if experience is the substance of evolution, then every day, every hour, every minute of our lives is an accomplishment of life purpose. We agonise unnecessarily over some life decisions, telling ourselves that there must be a right or wrong direction to take at each of life's crossroads. Sometimes we stay stuck at the crossroads, unable to read the signs or make a decision about which way to turn.

Influenced, as we are, by the Christian ethic (as interpreted by the Church), we imagine that the most effective lessons can only be learned through pain and suffering. We may shun what seems to be an easier path, even though we know it will lead to true joy and inner fulfilment. We have a tendency to see the Higher Authority, guides, higher selves, angels and spiritual helpers as demanding killjoys doling out nasty-tasting medicine, which nevertheless is bound to be better for us than medicine that is more palatable! Yet, once understood from a different perspective, the very mechanisms of karma and their interaction, not only with cause and effect, but also with the widening of incarnate experience, set us free to make freer and more creative decisions.

When making choices we must not forget that the highest potentials in life are associated with love, joy and compassion. Neither must we ignore the fact that, in the Western world, our principal religion has many contradictions. We can, it seems, in the same breath, speak of a God of love, forgiveness, mercy and compassion, who nevertheless requires 'an eye for an eye and a tooth for a tooth' – or perhaps several eyes for an eye and teeth for a tooth!

THE HIGHER PROCESS OF CHOICE

The process of making the choices for any given incarnation is complex. The life bead or grain, which we looked at in Chapter 2, returning to the thread or core, brings a record of the life that has just been lived, with all the positive causes (joys, glories, achievements and experience), as well as the negative causes (imbalances, mistakes, sins against the higher principles, conscious wrongdoings), which have been set in motion.

My own spiritual teacher (see Glossary) tells us that after death we go through a transition period. We spend time in a healing temple and are reunited with loved ones who are already on the 'other side'. But, when we have had time to adjust to our new state, we are required to make a detailed review and evaluation of the life we have just lived. We do this with support from more evolved guides, helpers and advisers, and with the benefit of the wider vision of the 'between life' state.

This experience has been described as similar to receiving deep psychotherapy. We are not judged, but we certainly judge ourselves as we see the effects and out-reaching nature of some of the ripples we have created in the lake of life. The causes and effects we have set in motion become very clear. The karmic choices for the next incarnation are based on this life review.

Each incarnating personality is essentially different. The exact being, which has returned, does not reincarnate. Another personality bead or grain takes up the baton and prepares to 'run' the next stage of the evolutionary marathon.

After the review, the soul thread, or core (the

consciousness of which is our higher self) decides the nature of the tasks to be undertaken by the next personality bead to incarnate. The self-recriminations of the returning personality bead may influence the choices of the higher self to take on heavy karmic burdens or obstacles in order to redress the balance.

Case Study: Janet

Janet had trained as a dancer. She was very gifted and felt that dance was her life. A few months after she had been 'noticed' and become a member of a touring dance company it had always been her ambition to join, she had a serious car accident. Her right leg was badly crushed. The surgeons, knowing she was a dancer, repaired it as carefully as they could. But, although she regained good movement and rehabilitated herself well, it became increasingly apparent that her leg would not stand up to weeks of travel, vigorous rehearsals and intensive performances. She was devastated that her promising career was over almost as soon as it had begun.

Janet went into therapy because of her overwhelming feelings of grief, depression, loss and despair. Though the therapy helped her through the darkest time and gave her the strength to consider what to do next with her life, she felt that she was an artist prevented from expressing her gift. Beyond her natural anger and frustration she began to feel the need to find some meaning and purpose from her accident and put it into some kind of context.

This search for meaning brought her to wide spiritual exploration. Meeting the concept of karma and other lifetimes seemed to speak to her. Maybe if she could understand the sequence of what had gone before, the loss of her ability to express her gift as she had hoped could also be understood and the way forward become clearer.

Until some therapy or self-growth work has been undertaken, it is unwise to seek regression to past lifetimes as a means of understanding present problems. Seeing all our difficulties as being rooted in past lives can all too easily become a means of escaping psychological insights relating to this present life and personality. But, when dealing with a blow such as Janet had encountered, looking into other lifetimes can be a relief and a release.

If the person is ready for past life insights, the way to uncovering them is rarely as difficult as it may seem. It does not require hypnosis, as such, to encourage someone as eager for the search as Janet was, to go into a state of deep relaxation and endeavour to 'see' or 'know' the events leading to the present experience.

In this deeply relaxed state Janet 'saw' another aspect of herself, in another lifetime. She felt that the landscape was Greek and that she was in an ancient world. Identifying with this other aspect she realised that she had been a trained dancer and gymnast. This 'Janet' of another lifetime was highly skilled and renowned, but as she recalled the atmosphere of this other existence, the present Janet felt that she did not much like this other self. She had been talented but arrogant. She was not a good team member. She wanted to be the one who was noticed, always the star.

Janet's Greek *alter ego* was supposed to help in training younger dancers, but she put them through punishing schedules and never gave praise. She seemed to be malicious towards others and intensely jealous of any who received too much praise and attention or threatened to take glory away from herself.

Several sessions spent getting in touch with this other

lifetime brought Janet to an understanding that in her present lifetime, in the here and now, she needed to resolve the imbalance in evolution caused by the Greek dancer. She saw this as a task for her soul. She was honest enough to admit that if her career in this lifetime had gone without a hitch, she could have become proud and egocentric too. She recognised that her accident could have ended in self-pity and resentment and have become an excuse for 'not getting on with life'.

Seeing another lifetime in this way is a deep experience. Janet needed time to process what she had felt and seen, and to make sure that what she had 'seen' resonated to her own deep sense of being 'on truth'. Eventually she decided that if she could not be a performing dancer she would become a teacher of dance and train and encourage the young. She had always felt that she knew more about dance than she had ever learned in this current lifetime and that she therefore had a great deal of knowledge to pass on.

In her teaching, Janet became known for her patience with struggling young dancers, especially if they were going through any crises in their training. After she had been teaching for some years she said:

> 'I might have turned to teaching dance, anyway, but it has been so important for me to do so from a place of understanding what had gone before. I am not just teaching because I cannot perform, I am doing it for the deeper purpose of paying an old debt and resolving an imbalance for my soul. I have learned to do it with joy and to consider it a privilege. I now see that what I once thought to be an unbearable loss and disaster has been an opening to something far greater in my life.'

KARMA, EVOLUTION AND THE HIGHER PRINCIPLES

Our interaction with the higher principles or archetypes of higher qualities is the main basis for karma and evolution (see also pages 20–1). We need to learn about each one of them. Our karmic choices will be activated by wishing to broaden our field of experience, as well as by our use or abuse of these principles and the need to balance that out. In this way each lifetime has a theme. The agenda given to a subsequently incarnating bead may, or may not, be directly related to the immediately previous life. We do not necessarily work on one theme, in linear fashion, until we have exhausted it. If, for instance, we have misused or abused the archetype of justice in a particular way, it might be several lifetimes later that an incarnating bead or grain picks up this specific redemptive or retributive task. The pattern of incarnation, karma and experience is serial but not necessarily linearly sequential. This means that one karmic theme is not necessarily followed sequentially through one lifetime after another without interruption, until it is completed. We may have several themes running at one and the same time so that the karma we are working with now does not always derive from the immediately preceding life. Some arising issues may require more deliberation at the soul level. Suitable incarnational openings and opportunities have to be carefully selected.

As a new soul bead prepares to incarnate, the higher self makes selections to ensure that the scene for optimum evolutionary experience is set. The geographical area, historical time and culture for the incarnation are chosen, as is the initial social milieu. Children choose their parents; parents choose their children. Gender, body type and mental orientation are also decided before physical conception takes place. Even the astrological influences at the moment of birth are chosen and directed.

The choice of these parameters belongs to the soul. The subsequent choices of the incarnating personality bead are therefore circumscribed. Certain choices will be impossible for the incarnate self to make, while any choice within the realms of possibility will lead to valuable experience needed by the soul for the building of evolution. In this way, destiny or pre-ordination, co-exist with free choice. Certain things are laid down but within those parameters the incarnate personality has much freedom to choose. It is up to the higher self to provide a field where, whatever subsequent choices the incarnate being makes, the requirements of karma and the broadening of experience will be served.

The full impact of this higher organisation means that, once incarnate, unless we deliberately, in full consciousness and responsibility, choose to flout the higher principles, *there are no wrong choices.* Each option we could possibly take leads to an experience we need, to further our evolution. The karmic law of cause and effect ensures that we gradually become more awake to, conscious and respectful of, the higher principles.

The ramifications of karma, choice and the organisation of the soul are so great, so complex to understand, that a series of images or pictorial illustrations may help.

BEADS ON A THREAD, GRAINS ON A CORE

I have already described (in Chapter 2) the basic arrangement of the soul, with the different aspects incarnating as beads on a thread, or grains on a core. If the thread of beads is imagined as a fastened necklace, this image can help us in moving away from linear or hierarchical models of evolution. The next bead in line is not necessarily the one to prepare for incarnation when a previous bead returns. It may be one from across the circle. In this way it is easier to recognise that karma is as much about breadth of experience as about resolving issues of immediate cause and effect. As each personality bead manifests into its own incarnation, it seeks evolutionary equilibrium for the whole, complex soul.

The current bead or grain in incarnation, may or may not have access to the wisdom or experience of the beads already returned to the thread or core. Evolution does not necessarily follow a novice/improver/expert/initiate sequence. Its progression depends upon breadth of experience, wholeness and consciousness, rather than ignorance/innocence, through tutoring to perfection. This means that much of our karmic programme, certainly in the earlier stages of unfolding, deals with polarities. Each incarnating bead is a distinct and, in many ways, self-governing universe. Qualities to experience in incarnation may be *chosen*, rather than being arrived at through steady learning. It may be that, having experienced what it is to be wise, we decide to learn what it is to be foolish as a way of balancing things out and guarding against hubris. In this way foolishness does not necessarily come first and wisdom after. Gentleness does not inevitably succeed violence, love follow hate or creativity go after destruction. Every experience has its place in a whole, which we can only ever partially comprehend with the finite mind.

ACTORS IN THE WINGS

In his play, *As You Like It*, William Shakespeare wrote:

> All the world's a stage,
> And all the men and women merely players:
> They have their exits and their entrances;
> And one man in his time plays many parts ...

A good analogy for incarnation and karmic intentions is that of the stage on which we all act. To a degree, before incarnation, we stand in the wings of a giant stage, writing our script and choosing the other actors who will play out life's dramas and comedies with us.

THE CHESSBOARD OF LIFE

Though a giant hand does not play us like pieces on a chessboard there is nevertheless a chessboard element to the logistics involved in our life choices. At the higher self level, we choose our own chessboard, our own pieces and the state of play upon it. We choose which of the chess pieces is to be our identity for any given lifetime, and thus the pattern and nature of the moves we are able to make.

WEAVING A RICH TAPESTRY

Another helpful image is that of the tapestry. The overall vision of the whole tapestry is held by the individual soul or group soul (see below, page 49). The colours and particular stitch patterns are chosen by the weaver at the work face, and are more subject to the conscious choice of each incarnate individual – the living, breathing, feeling, knowing *you* or *I*.

From the soul or higher self level, certain co-weavers are also chosen. The patterns, then interwoven, form the fabric of life. The tapestry, produced by the interactions, is eternally present yet unfolding at subtle levels of awareness. Individuals and groups of individuals weave separate parts of the tapestry and only gradually does our vision extend so that we glimpse the complex whole, own our part in it, and so weave our threads more consciously into the total pattern. Learning to weave and interweave our threads into the pattern with greater consciousness is the goal of evolution and the main reason why karma exists.

As we interlace our own particular thread in this vast tapestry of life it is inevitable that we shall feel frequently as though we are weaving blind. It is not easy to maintain either a vision of what we are personally creating or of what has been, and is being created, at wider and wider levels. We may sense that we have a place in the cosmic pattern, yet have enormous difficulty in divining exactly what that place may be. We tend to exist in a 'cloud of unknowing'. Becoming frustrated with the 'unknowing' is a sign that we are choosing to be more conscious. When we are ready to look, we learn how to read the clues, which help us more clearly to divine and define the path of our personal thread and its part in the karmic pattern.

As previously discussed, the soul structure is complex. The beads on the necklace or grains on the core are an integral group or community. Souls also belong to soul families or soul groups. The following imagery may help in understanding this.

TREES AND FORESTS

Imagine a tree, then the forest where it stands; then many other forests of trees. The twigs, leaves and fruits that spring from the same branch are soul families. The tree, with all its branches and offshoots, is a soul group. The forest containing the trees is a wider soul group. In life we meet those who are from the same branch as ourselves, those who are from the same tree and those who are from the same forest, as well as those who are from completely different forests. When we meet close members of our soul family we often recognise them joyfully, as soul mates, feeling ourselves to be of similar 'substance' with them. Members of our genetic family may or may not be members of our close soul family. (The concept of twin souls is discussed on page 75.)

Many people who come for help from my spiritual teacher and discarnate guide, Gildas, or for therapy, express a sadness about their family of origin. 'I seem different from the rest of my family'; 'I know my parents love me in their own way, but they don't understand me'; 'I feel that I don't belong'; 'I feel unseen and unheard'; 'I respect my family, but somehow I don't seem to be of the same substance as them'.

Society and religion exhort us to love our families. When we don't find this easy, or feel unloved by other family members, great grief, poor self-image and puzzlement can result. It can be a great relief to recognise that genetic and true spiritual family may not be one and the same thing. As we go through life we meet people with whom we have close affinities. For some of us these affinities seem to go far deeper than the familial experience. If we understand that we choose our genetic family to help forward our karmic purpose and evolution, and might therefore not be born to parents who are close soul mates, many feelings of guilt and bewilderment can drop away. We can more readily see our family of origin with tenderness and understanding as co-travellers, with their own karmic agenda, and rejoice with those others we meet in life and recognise as being more truly and spiritually close than our family of origin.

Where soul and genetic family coincide there is an added bonus, but those who are very close to us may also be our most challenging teachers. When setting the stage for our incarnations, we may ask loved ones, who will incarnate concurrently, to make sure we learn necessary lessons, even if the role they take on to expedite that learning is a difficult one for all concerned. (See also pages 73–4.)

EVOLUTIONARY CONCERNS

Evolution is the process of more fully learning the nature of the higher principles and becoming adept at manifesting these in the manner of our living and relationships. Much karma and karmic choice, then, is connected to these. In the process of naming and understanding higher principles we create archetypes. (See also pages 20–1 and the Glossary.) Through even a basic understanding of archetypes we can gain more insight into the organisation of our karma and bring the nature of our present life purposes and overall choices more fully to consciousness.

The sum total of the choices made by the higher self for a particular incarnation includes the evolutionary lessons to be learned, the karma to be repaid, the imbalances to be rectified and the service we may elect to give to humanity or the Earth. To ensure the accomplishment of these multi-faceted aims, our higher selves endeavour to involve us particularly with one or more of the higher principles or archetypes. Identifying the archetypal umbrella, under which we live, enables us to co-operate more totally with the purposes of our higher selves and to further our evolution and spiritual fulfilment more actively and with greater awareness.

Each of us, on coming into incarnation, carries as a gift or message from our higher selves, an 'incoming will to . . .'. This may remain relatively unconscious, particularly if we have taken on a heavy burden of retributive/repentant karma (see page 56). Yet it is possible to make this knowledge conscious, and in so doing to recognise the key or touchstone that will enable us to surmount the retributive/repentant obstacles. Once we sense, and actively work with, the principles or archetypes pertaining to our incoming will, the whole of life becomes more congruent and our karma begins to take care of itself.

There are higher, pure archetypes, degraded archetypes and shadow archetypes, all related to karma and karmic learning. The key words describing the nature of our 'incoming will to . . .' are derived from the list of higher principles or pure archetypes. No suggested list can be comprehensive. In order to align ourselves with our higher motivation we need to seek the key words that really motivate and speak to us at a personal level and give us that 'Aha!' sense of discovery. This means that any given list will have room within it for creativity. There will always be additional words, close to the meaning of others, yet more pertinent or meaningful to a particular individual.

KEY WORDS FOR LIFE

For some, the key word will be more straightforward and easily related to the basic list of pure archetypal qualities. For others it will be more elusive or subtle, requiring considerable thought or meditation in order to arrive at the one word truly enlivening to, or encapsulating of, our inner sense of life purpose.

The following is a list of suggested key words to be used in completing the phrase 'the incoming will to ...'. They arise from the higher principles or pure archetypes of higher qualities (see pages 20–1). Some words appear in more than one list, as the archetypes can engender similar qualities. Yet, it is subtly, but importantly different to have chosen to work with creativity under the archetype of love than to have elected to work with creativity under the archetype of power. Each has its place; one is not better than the other, but they fulfil a different purpose.

• From the higher archetype of *Love* comes love of God, love of others, love of self-sacrifice, tenderness, mothering, nurturing, caring, creativity, dedication, vocation, commitment, healing, love of earth and growing things, love of animals, conservation, transformation, giving, contentment.

• From the higher archetype of *Justice* comes equality, fairness, administration, law, order, guardianship, authority, leadership, reform, social conscience, politics, mitigation, arbitration, warriorship, human rights, debate, caring, idealism.

• From the higher archetype of *Peace* comes peace-making, warriorship, arbitration, citizenship, defence, guardianship, healing, planning, order, freedom, relating, union, humanitarianism, safety, prayer, meditation, quietude.

• From the higher archetype of *Beauty* comes preservation, creativity, shaping, artistry, skill, observation, grace, transformation, appreciation, colour, design, architecture, building, vision, assessment, perspective, awareness.

• From the higher archetype of *Harmony* comes music, creativity, peace-making, dance, art, colour, design, symmetry, arbitration, counselling, inner searching, healing, friendship, empathy, rhythm, understanding, tolerance.

• From the higher archetype of *Power* comes rulership, leadership, teaching, priesthood, government, self-empowerment, empowerment of others, self-actualisation (see also Glossary), ambition, initiating, competitiveness, acquisition, responsibility, direction, inspiration, vision, hope, dedication, idealism, belief, courage, confidence, law and order, competence.

• From the higher archetype of *Service* comes dedication, purpose, serving others, service of religion, pastoral care, vision for humanity, responsibility, administration, law and order, transformation, transmutation, healing, counselling, giving, self-sacrifice, social conscience, belief, social reform, improvement, idealism, patriotism, humanitarianism, love of others.

• From the higher archetype of *Wholeness* comes self-growth, equality, balance, inclusiveness, healing, perception, blending, acceptance, seeking, exploration, assimilation, completion, vision, tolerance, breadth of knowledge, symbolism, creativity.

• From the higher archetype of *Perfection* comes idealism, God consciousness, dedication, striving, healing, endeavour, vision, stoicism, industriousness, seeking the highest, goodness, belief, setting standards, aims, goal-setting, confidence, focus, advising, leadership, artistry, worth, conservation, preservation, following a prescribed path closely, application, diligence.

Pondering on the key words or higher archetypes that speak to you, inspire or move you, helps in finding a clearer sense of why you are here, what some of your karmic tasks may be and more fully understanding and harmonising with the purposes of your higher self.

We are a *doing*-oriented society. Evolution and therefore karma are concerned with wholeness and balance of experience. Care must be taken to ensure that the key words are also considered in relationship to lifestyles that are potentially more *being*-oriented. Creating and maintaining a beautiful home or garden or mothering are, at one level, very active and demanding tasks, yet it is the happy homemaker's quality of being that deeply touches others. Some people also know that the actual nature of the work they do is less important than the quality of being they are able to bring to it. Some people learn to *be* through *doing*; others learn to *do* through *being*.

Because the higher principles have a complex inter-relationship they cannot be over-simplistically separated from one another. A life where the theme is service may also teach us about wholeness, justice or love and vice versa. If we are over-dedicated to one particular archetype or obsessional about it, we may unconsciously create imbalances in our ability to honour some of the others. Such imbalances set causes in action and produce the effects needing to be corrected through karmic choice and compensation.

Higher principles and archetypes are dynamic forces affecting the whole of life, living and relating. In our struggle to learn, we both degrade the archetypes and box with their shadows. By doing this we enable ourselves to comprehend the abstract and eventually to separate out the pure from the pseudo-archetype or the stereotype. Thus, in life, instead of dealing directly with wholeness we may, for example, create or suffer from separatism, racism or purism. (As degraded archetypes these are the 'separatist', the 'racist' and the 'purist'.)

The most encompassing higher principle or archetype is that of power. Through evolution we come fully into our own power or empowerment. Therefore, over and over again, in different ways, from different angles and different perspectives, we all encounter the degraded or semi-degraded archetypes of power: tyrant, witch, magician, dictator, controller, ruler, guru, teacher, leader. Each of these creates an opposite or counterpart. The tyrant creates the victim (or the victim creates the tyrant); the witch, the bewitched; the magician, the entranced or duped; the dictator, the doormat; the controller, the spineless, the rebel; the ruler, the subject; the guru, the devotee; the teacher, the pupil; the leader, the follower.

RETRIBUTION, REDEMPTION AND TRANSCENDENCE

As in the process of evolution we encounter all these energies and manifestations so our karma is formed and enacted. There are three main karmic stages or phases: *retribution/ repentance, redemption* and *transcendence*.

The retributive/repentant stage of karma is not necessarily an exacting or punitive retribution for sins of omission or commission. It is the phase when, in response to the overview and vision of the higher self, our eternal beings become conscious of the necessity to make retribution or repentance for imperfections, imbalances and failures to live responsibly in accordance with the higher principles or archetypes. Retributive/repentant karma is often concerned with polarities.

In any given lifetime retribution/repentance should be a transitional stage. It is the one that accounts for many of the obstacles, blockages or apparent unfairnesses, which we observe as occurring right from the start of our lives, simply by the 'accident' of our birth. The more we understand karma to be not only a law of cause and effect, but also a law of choice, the more can we realise that the circumstances into which we incarnate are neither 'sentence' nor 'accident', but exist as the result of careful selection.

Janet, in the case history on page 41, saw her accident as retributive/repentant karma. It altered the direction of her life and served to make her conscious of her life purpose in a totally new way. As she turned her talents to teaching, and when she learned to see her accident as a 'gift', she also came to know the meaning of redemptive and transcendent karma.

The redemptive stage of karma is often characterised by a need to serve or to find an active purpose in life. We may become very aware of the importance of one or more of the higher principles or archetypes and find realisation in working to implement such higher values in our own and others' lives. In the true redemptive stage of karma the obstacles, blockages and challenges of the retributive stage are fully accepted, used positively, surmounted or transformed.

Transcendent karma is more difficult to describe. Synonyms for the word 'transcend' are surpass, exceed, rise above, go beyond, excel, outrival, outlive, outstrip, outdo, eclipse and outshine. Synonyms for 'transcendent' are surpassing, exceeding, matchless, peerless, unrivalled, unparalleled, incomparable, supreme and consummate. Adjectives deriving from these words are transcendental, supernatural, mystical, abstract and metaphysical. From this list the sense in which transcendent almost always conveys something of the spiritual and metaphysical can be fully appreciated.

In terms of explaining or understanding transcendent karma the most useful synonyms are surpassing, exceeding, going beyond and rising above. In the phase of retributive karma we aim to make ourselves conscious of the effect of causes we have set into motion. In the phase of redemptive karma we do service to balance our past imperfections. In the phase of transcendent karma we surpass ourselves, exceed the service, which may have been required, and eventually go beyond and rise above it. At the retributive and redemptive stages there is a certain bondage to the original cause and its effect. At the transcendent stage the bondage is over, the balance made, the lesson assimilated, the way forward clearer. Transcendent karma is associated with consciousness.

To some extent these three phases or stages of karma are linear and hierarchical in sequence, yet they also co-exist or operate alongside each other, especially at the retributive and redemptive stages. The ground rules of life are intricate. We work on more than one piece of karma in any given span. So, for any one individual, some life issues may be at the retributive stage, others at the redemptive stage and yet others at the transcendent state.

At the retributive/redemptive stage of karma usually we will be very conscious of obstacles or blockages to our progress through life. It is these very obstacles that help us to see the circumscription chosen by our higher selves and to learn to accept it. This acceptance will help us to focus on, and develop, the very things required to further our overall learning and karmic purpose. An illustration from my own life may help to bring theory closer to practice or experience.

I have always had vivid dreams about being adept at riding difficult or fiery horses, running long distances and climbing high mountains with ease. In this lifetime my body lacks the sort of co-ordination or agility that makes such feats possible. I am not good at any sport. My attempts to learn to ride even the most well-mannered of horses have ended in quite serious falls. I *have* tried to push these particular boundaries more than once but eventually have had to accept that my present talents lie more in the direction of communication, teaching, counselling, healing, writing and being a channel for my guide (see Glossary).

Being unable to ride and without physical prowess is not a heavy, retributive karma in itself but these lacks have been emphasised by certain other life choices or events. I was born into a family where such things were highly valued. I married a man who excelled at sports and who came to despise my ineptitude. An appreciation of, and contentment with, the gifts chosen for me in this lifetime only came when I learned to value service to others. I sense that in some other lifetime I had pursued sport and physical prowess for its own sake and neglected other duties and commitments. It could also be that I have often, in other lifetimes, had opportunities to excel physically and, this time around, needed complementary experience. The body I am in has cut off the way to unnecessary repetition, and made me develop other faculties and appreciate other values.

An alternative way of reparation might have been to choose a sporty body and then to use sport as a service rather than in the narcissistic way I sense I used it previously. But this would have meant a delay for my soul in broadening its overall range of incarnate experience.

Karma is like a dance or a series of dances. It takes two to tango! It takes many more than two to do elaborate formation or set dances. By the very nature of our interactions as human beings karma goes beyond the personal. The next chapter examines more closely some of the implications of the choices made by our higher selves and also looks at the concepts of group karma, family karma, racial karma, the karma of humanity, karmic debt, karmic enmeshment and instant karma.

Before moving on to the next chapter, you may like to complete the following meditative exercise. Its aim is to help you to identify the key words that are important for you in this lifetime.

Exercise 4: Meditatively or Intuitively Considering Your Key Words for this Lifetime

This is a reflective, meditative exercise to help you to get insight into the personal application of the key words and archetypes described on pages 52–4. Read these pages again before you begin and maybe make a check list to have at hand during this contemplation.

Make sure that you will be undisturbed and that you have writing and drawing materials at hand. Sit or lie down for this exercise. Arrange your body symmetrically. Sit cross-legged or in a lotus position if you wish, but otherwise, whether seated on a chair or lying down, do not cross your legs at the knees or ankles. Your head should be in alignment with your spine and well-balanced or supported if you are in a sitting position.

Close your eyes and become aware of your breathing. Gradually let it find its own rhythm, without forcing or trying to breathe in any special way. Your natural, relaxed breath rhythm will help you to feel calm and quiet and to turn your attention inward.

Imagine that there is a gentle source of light above the crown of your head. This is a healing and inspirational light. Feel it expanding around you like a cloak of golden light. Let the light penetrate each part, each cell of your body, bringing you warmth, light and healing . . .

Reflectively consider the life and purpose key words, opening your eyes to refer briefly to your check list if you wish. Get a feeling of the things in life that feed your creativity and sense of fulfilment. Ask yourself what you feel may be missing from your life. Ask that any words or symbols that will enable you to be clearer about your sense of purpose in this lifetime may come into your mind . . .

After five to ten minutes, gradually let the light fade. Become aware of your body on the chair or the floor; feel your connection with the earth; visualise a cloak of light with a hood around you, so that you are not too open and vulnerable, and also take light with you wherever you go.

Make any notes or drawings to help you to remember your experiences during this meditation. Be aware that you may need to repeat it several times on different occasions before you get the answers or certainties you are looking for.

Chapter 4

KARMIC CLUES IN THE WIDE AND COLOURFUL TAPESTRY OF LIFE

That is its painting on the glorious clouds,
And these its emeralds on the peacock's train;
It hath its stations in the stars; its slaves
In lightning, wind and rain . . .

THE DILEMMA OF NON-REMEMBRANCE • THE KARMIC PATTERN
OR BLUEPRINT • KARMIC CLUES • OUR GENETIC INHERITANCE
• CHOOSING IMPERFECTION • CHOICE OF GENDER •
POLARITIES AS AN AID TO UNDERSTANDING • CHOICE OF
PARENTS • THE TRUE SELF • KARMIC BUSINESS – PUTTING
THINGS RIGHT • THE PERFECT PARTNER OR TWIN SOUL •
THE SPLITTING OF THE ORIGINAL SPARK • KARMIC THEMES
AND TRIGGERS • EVOLUTIONARY CHALLENGES AND
RE-PRESENTATIONS • EXERCISE 5 IDENTIFYING KARMIC
THEMES REPRESENTED BY LIFE'S POLARITIES AND
FRUSTRATIONS • EXERCISE 6 GETTING OFF THE TREADMILL

This chapter explains more about soul families, groups and
twin souls. It outlines some of the karmic challenges of life

and the way in which we may implement them for ourselves. As you read, in order to get a clearer sense of your own karmic choices or tasks, keep your own life review in mind. (See Exercise 1 on page 22.)

THE DILEMMA OF NON-REMEMBRANCE

Few people spontaneously remember their past lives. As we become aware of the implications of karma, it may seem strange that we do not have access, while on Earth, to our previous records. Yet to have that access would take away spontaneity and a great deal of individuality. Once we know where the pieces in a jigsaw fit, the puzzle may lose its interest! To know our past lives and our exact karmic debts might lead us to create more negative karma rather than less, since pride, false humility, escapism or over-compensation could so easily get in the way. It would be too easy for us to be little *other* than actors on a stage, cut off from the true immediacy of our deepest emotions, thoughts and interactions.

THE KARMIC PATTERN OR BLUEPRINT

Each one of us carries a unique combination of physical, mental, emotional and spiritual attributes. Among biologists, philosophers, psychologists and clergy, arguments abound about whether it is nature or nurture that determines our individuality. The karmic standpoint is that we make an overview of our psychological opportunities and challenges, bring with us our eternal but individualised spirit and choose our gender and genetic inheritance, including genetic intelligence and biochemistry. In choosing or overseeing the circumstances into which we shall incarnate, a karmic pattern or blueprint is laid down from the soul level.

KARMIC CLUES

Instead of knowing what our programme is, we have to search for clues, follow intuitions and hunches, ponder on relationships, question all exchanges and learn the unwritten rules of karma by seeking spiritual awareness. The *details* of other lifetimes and the search for proof that 'I' existed in ancient Egypt, Greece or eighteenth-century London are rarely relevant. It is a recognition of the themes, the dynamics and the archetypes we are learning about or serving that can best help us to understand our karma and hence, consciously, to further our evolution.

We all have extremes in our lives, perhaps even tendencies we dislike in ourselves and would wish to eradicate. We may be obsessively tidy or unable to create order at all; we may live frugally or extravagantly, by compulsion; we may hoard food for fear of running out or prefer to keep our cupboards comparatively empty and shop from day to day. We may love food or fear it – or have a love/hate relationship with it. Most of us have at least one irrational fear – of snakes, spiders, the dark, enclosed spaces or large open spaces, people walking behind us, heights, caves, fire or water.

If we are open to the concept of reincarnation, sudden or spontaneous realisations about other lives may put a different context on these extremes or fears. Seeing them in a different light, they may lose some of the power they can have over us. This can happen without the need for formal regression into other times.

Case Study: Tabitha

Tabitha, working on her need to horde food and her inability to leave anything uneaten on her plate, was born during the war years. Food was precious, and almost everyone tried to keep something special in the food cupboard for a birthday celebration or in case rationing became even more stringent. Parents exhorted their children to eat everything they were given. Waste was not to be tolerated. All these attitudes were in Tabitha's conscious memory bank for this current lifetime. Yet she could not sustain any change in her attitude to food. Then in one therapy session she said, almost lightheartedly 'Perhaps I starved to death in another lifetime'.

I took her 'throwaway' remark very seriously, though. 'Perhaps you did' was all I said. There was a long silence, after which Tabitha said, 'I do believe that is what this is all about. I am afraid of starvation. Much more deeply than any war experience of shortages can account for. If there is not enough, I fear for my life. When food is there, I must make sure to eat all of it.'

Over the next couple of weeks Tabitha's certainty became clearer. She could see herself, probably in Europe, in the Middle Ages, a young girl, begging for her living. She felt that her family had been wiped out by some disease, maybe smallpox or the plague. She had survived the disease, but had no one to take her in. She literally starved to death.

The vision was stark but the understanding it brought was deep. Now she could observe her own tendency with real compassion and could calm her fears by reminding herself that this life was very different from that other one.

Gradually balance came. The symptom had told its story and so it no longer had control over her.

Case Study: Martin

Martin had to dress formally for his work where the dress code decreed smart suits, shirts and ties. He loved his work, but found that a dislike of things being tight around his neck was turning to panic proportions, and becoming more and more troublesome. He was wearing a larger collar size than he really needed and trying not to tie his necktie too tight, but still the symptoms persisted. Sometimes he would have to go off to the lavatory to loosen his clothing and take a 'breather'. On one or two occasions he had caught himself beginning to hyperventilate.

Symptoms of this kind can relate to a difficult birth, perhaps to an experience of the baby having the umbilical cord round its neck. I asked him to find out whether his birth had been traumatic, but his mother, when questioned, said he had been born easily after quite a short labour.

When I asked Martin to try to name what his panic was about he said, 'I seem to be afraid of being strangled. I'm afraid of dying by being strangled.'

The possibility of other lifetimes and the effects they can have on our current lives was comparatively new to Martin. But after I suggested, 'Perhaps you have died by strangulation in another time and place', his panics about his shirt and tie became less. He would probably never enjoy wearing anything tight or too close to his neck, but the feelings were no longer out of hand. Even being able to say, when the symptoms threatened, that this may be a memory from another time, brought relief and enabled him to focus on the immediate present.

When we diligently search and are open to the potential of the working hypothesis, inner certainties grow and our lives can become enhanced by the sense of having a true spiritual direction, which is within our care and control.

OUR GENETIC INHERITANCE

One of the biggest sets of clues to our karmic direction and purpose lies in the body we are in. (See reference to my personal story on pages 57–9.) We choose our parents and therefore our genetic inheritance. Our bodies and minds predispose us to be able, or not, to follow certain directions. To a large extent our genetic inheritance determines the areas in which our gifts and talents lie or, at least, the areas in which we have a likelihood of success or failure.

At various times, society urges the need for more scientists, artists, teachers, doctors, farmers, nurses, linguists, social workers, sportsmen and women or engineers. Employment opportunities may form patterns with anything from policing, through service, retail, manual labour, agriculture, management or care-work being in the ascendant.

Too often we try to mould ourselves to fit these imposed needs or to fulfil the expectations and aspirations of parents and teachers. Yet the bottom line is that we are hardly likely to become successful brain surgeons if our bodies, minds and predispositions fit us better for tree-felling or road-building. The raw material we bring with us can be trained, honed, manicured and perfected, but limitations or frustrated talents will inevitably make themselves felt. Yet opposition can make us more conscious of our true selves. We often learn best what we really want by knowing what we don't want; or who we really are, by knowing who we are not. Karmically, we *choose* opposition as part of our repentance, but also in order to make us aware and self-determining.

CHOOSING IMPERFECTION

Knowing we have chosen certain oppositions at the soul level can set us on the journey to finding out *why* we selected a certain genetic inheritance. It can be difficult enough to come to terms with bodily or mental factors, which fall within the bounds of normality. How much more difficult is it then, within a framework of karmic belief, to divine reasons why a body that is truly abnormal or disabled may be chosen or why we might genetically inherit a severe or life-limiting disease. Yet to reflect that such a trial may have to be chosen as part of evolutionary planning may make more sense, or be more constructive than to reflect why such a condition could have been meted out to us, or forced upon us by a judgemental authority.

Reasons for choosing a physically challenging incarnation are wide in their range and implication. Understanding them means holding in mind that one aspect of karma is related to gaining breadth of experience. Being in a disabled body involves learning a mixture of dependence and independence, and in the evolutionary spectrum these are important polarities. The well-rounded being is neither fiercely nor aggressively independent, nor severely dependent and unable to function *unless* there are props and support. Therefore, disablement might be seen as one way of both experiencing and resolving these polarities.

Parents of sick, disabled, physically or mentally challenged children often speak of the learning they manifest for others. Living in the moment is something to which many of us may spiritually aspire but find eternally difficult. Yet those we have tended to term 'handicapped' often show us the way to such a state of being. They also teach us about compassion, the art of graceful dependency and the pitfalls for the over-eager helper. The title of the former *Does He Take Sugar?* programme on BBC Radio 4 says it all!

CHOICE OF GENDER

One of the most important choices for each incarnation is our choice of gender. When we consider that it is the incoming being who makes such choices, rather than the parents anxious to conceive, a whole new perspective is thrown on to the current trend of some parents wanting to choose the gender of their children before conception.

The beads on the thread and the grains on the core are not basically gender carrying, though each core or strand will be predominantly yin or yang (see Glossary and page 75 on Twin souls). The Western practice of using the words 'masculine' and 'feminine' followed by 'principle' to describe the supreme interactive creative forces leads to confusion. 'Masculine' is 'man' or 'male' and 'feminine' is 'woman' or 'female'. The principles of creation are marginalised if, as a result of such narrow semantics, we confuse them with the socially conditioned behaviours of man and woman. The Chinese words yin and yang, and the symbol associated with them, makes for a fuller understanding and a less biased approach.

Yin and yang are the basic, opposite, yet united forces of creation. Yin is receptive, yielding and dark. Yang is active, thrusting and light. In the traditional yin/yang symbol one black and one white fish-like shape nestle together to form a perfect circle. The eye of the black shape is white and that of the white shape black, showing that the seed of each is contained in the other.

During evolution it is important that we gain experience of both yin and yang, as well as of the challenges, opportunities and oppositions that are consequent upon male or female gender.

POLARITIES AS AN AID TO UNDERSTANDING

Whether we look to our bodies or to our physical, mental or emotional environment for clues, the need to experience but then to transcend polarities is a major guideline to understanding our karmic choices. Understanding the polarity pulls in our lives, gives us a key that unlocks the way forward and empowers the choices of the incarnate personality.

CHOICE OF PARENTS

Many of the encumbrances or opportunities we encounter in seeking to find our true selves and our harmonious expression into life are also largely the result of our choice of parents. Choosing to whom we shall be born also takes care of the *where, when* and *into which strata of social opportunity* we will incarnate. These play a great part in determining our psychological and emotional environment, as also do the characters, drives and life experiences of our parents and forebears.

Societies are subject to trends and fashions. Geographical areas are associated with different religions, belief systems, legal structures and educational methods. Today some countries, or parts of them, are highly sophisticated, mechanised, materially oriented and computerised, while other areas are simple and undeveloped, with life lived basically and frugally. The materially 'advanced' communities have labelled the 'backward' ones as 'the third world'. Richness and poverty are seen mainly in monetary terms, and 'quality of life', is seen as totally dependent upon material possessions and sophisticated transport. Values, issues of self-worth and power are karmically fertile areas.

Collective and geographic values are powerful in shaping some aspects of character and personality, but human beings also have qualities of soul and spirit that shape our interactions with what *is*, at any given moment, and that hold the secrets of success. Those who live creatively do so against the background of their times and cultures, but not as victims of them. Spiritual awareness and a vision of human potential aid creative living and spell death to the archetype of the victim or conformist.

The parents we choose may be slaves of their environment. Children of such parents may recognise this and struggle to be free. The struggle will often be intensified where we have chosen our parents more for genetic reasons than because they are members of our soul family. Parents may also, at the higher preview level, decide to 'invite' into incarnation, children who will be their harsh taskmasters in the school of evolutionary and karmic learning.

There is no doubt that children thrive best when given unconditional love and support. But where closeness and recognition are missing, there are immediate life lessons, which usually have a karmic significance, to be learned. The spiritual picture is always wider and more complex than the social expectations. Seeking the wider picture enables us to understand *why* we are different, rather than feeling that it is *wrong* to be different. The urge to find out true selves and the permission to do so enables us to work through the difficult stage of retributive/repentant karma (see page 56). Families often, albeit unwittingly at the here and now level, provide the necessary obstacles that kick-start the repentant/retributive experience (see also page 73).

THE TRUE SELF

Each of us has a true self. Many of the conditioning mechanisms of society and parenting prevent the true self seed from flourishing. This is especially true where society or its pervading religions do not recognise a basic continuity of being, at the spirit and soul level. Belief in life after death is not enough. Only a belief in life or consciousness before birth can help to foster a sense of wonder and respect for the true seed or blueprint in each one of us.

When gardening, we take care to put our plants into the amalgam of soil and environment, which we know will encourage them to grow as well as possible. We note whether our seedlings like to be reasonably dry or well watered; we transplant them if they are too crowded or do not have enough light and shade to enable them to grow.

If we grow seeds or plants that have lost their labels, we watch, with interest, their reactions to the environment in which we have put them. We endeavour to discover what suits them best. When they fruit or flower we accept what they produce, knowing that the plant contains a blueprint and that we cannot influence poppy seeds to become cucumbers or force plants of unknown origin to produce what we *will* them to produce.

Our society is complex and stereotyped. Children are often, symbolically, if not actually, force-fed, starved of stimulus, strenuously moulded and denied choice and individuality; they are required to fit 'convenient' structures. All these things mean that at some time in our lives many of us will need help or counselling, at the psychological level, in order to find empowerment and satisfactory direction. At the karmic level these obstacles are our teachers. The journey to inner 'permission' to be positively who we are reflects the transition from retributive/repentant to redemptive karma (see also pages 56–8).

KARMIC BUSINESS – PUTTING THINGS RIGHT

Beyond the genetic, psychological and social environment provided by our choice of parents and siblings, we may, or may not, have direct karmic business with them as individuals. When we have got things wrong for each other in previous lifetimes we can choose to come together again in order to put things right. Because polarities help us to consciousness, 'putting things right' might involve an exaggerated swing of the pendulum. Where a parent has been harsh and restrictive to a child in one incarnation, these two beings might be drawn together in a subsequent incarnation, once more as parent and child. If the pendulum swings too far, the child may be given too few boundaries and become insecure because of that. An alternative personal interaction might be for the parent to become the child in the subsequent incarnation and either experience being given over-rigid boundaries, or a complete lack of holding and concern.

Difficult karma between two people does not necessarily indicate that they are from different soul groups or spiritual families. We all have to learn the lessons, which we can only teach each other. The image of actors in the wings preparing to come on to the stage of life shows how part of our choices for incarnation may be actually to arrange for someone to personify for us the very lesson we need to learn. Two people who find it difficult to get along together in life, may be close soul family, committed so strongly to each other's evolution that they are willing to go through such an enactment with all the lack of existential recognition it involves. These enactments are always very powerful. They are not passing difficulties in life, but often struggles that leave a deep imprint and that are not easily forgotten or forgiven within the lifespan that encompasses them.

We may, of course, also choose harmonious family circumstances. That which we all hold as the model – a family in which there is a common sense of spiritual recognition and purpose – is the ideal. Not all karma is negative and when we are living lives where service may be a primary purpose, the choice of a family that will bring out the best in us, makes sense. We must also remember that happiness is a karmic goal. If we stay too close to definitions of karma as a law that involves a great deal of punishment and reward, we tend to focus on suffering, repentance and penitence rather than on happiness and contentment as indicators to our path and purpose in life.

We all have a strong need to search for a place of belonging. This need may be intensified, if we suspect that instead of seeking to come into incarnation surrounded by those who are of the same spiritual substance as ourselves, we chose our family of origin for genetic purposes or to furnish the requirements of the retributive/penitent stage of karma (see also page 56).

We may meet up with friends in life who feel spiritually closer to us than our family of origin ever could. Many people feel guilty about such attachments and links, fearing to betray loyalties to those who, when all is said and done, have usually not only birthed us but also sheltered, nurtured, raised and loved us to the best of their abilities. A wider spiritual perspective, which helps us to see that genetic family members are not necessarily spiritual family, can help in the many instances where divided loyalties arise.

Our pre-life karmic and evolutionary choices usually include having some true spiritual companions in incarnation at the same time as us. When these choices have been made, there is a wondrous synchronicity which ensures that our paths in life will cross, usually at a mutually optimum moment.

THE PERFECT PARTNER OR TWIN SOUL

As well as the need to find a sense of true spiritual family, most of us nurture the longing to find our perfect partner, twin spark or twin soul. Although the desire to find union with a perfect partner is active within most of us, the definition of what our spiritual relationship to such a partner may be is more elusive. So far, in defining the nature and complexity of the soul in order to envisage the workings of karma more clearly, the illustrations of beads on a thread or grains on a core have been used, and family and group souls have been described as trees and forests. In order to understand the position of the twin soul we need to re-visit, and add to, the working definition of how human souls originate (see pages 34–6).

THE SPLITTING OF
THE ORIGINAL SPARK

A human soul is a spark, which splits off from the Source and chooses human incarnation as its destiny. As it begins its journey of evolution, which will, eventually, lead it back to the Source, the spark partially splits once more. The yin, or feminine of its essence, splits from the yang, or masculine (see Glossary for further definition of yin and yang). These two essences will take different but complementary and inter-dependent journeys. Each part is like a stem of corn joined at the root or like two strands on a beaded necklace joined at the fastening. The beads on each strand of the necklace, or the grains on each core of corn, represent opportunities for incarnation. The grains from the yin stem or beads from the yin strand will not always undergo or choose feminine incarnation, nor will those from the yang essence always take on a masculine body but, at the deepest level, they will always carry a stronger yin or yang imprint.

The main Divine Principle is that of creation. Yin and yang energies interacting together bring about the birth of the new. Part of the purpose of evolution for human beings is to understand, experience and, therefore, use in a balanced way, these sacred and divine energies. The taking on of a gender is one of the ways in which this learning happens. Since each stem or strand is slanted towards one principle or the other, and since it is possible for twin souls and soul aspects to meet in incarnation bearing the same gender, homosexuality takes on a different connotation. From a spiritual standpoint these things are part of experience, part of exploration, not manifestations which need to be judged or categorically ruled as abnormal, unnatural or dangerous.

In life, the longing for the twin soul is well known. When evolution is complete, which means that all the beads on each thread or core have incarnated and returned, the two strands or stems will become one again. During incarnation, until that is possible, a grain from one stem or a bead from one thread may meet with a flower or bead from its twin essence. When such a meeting happens, the twin souldom or perfect partnership is recognised and experienced.

Yet, twin souls do not always incarnate at the same time. It is highly likely that we will *not* meet or mate with our twin spark. There are other close and satisfying spiritual family or soul group partnerships that are possible and that, sometimes, we must learn not to spoil or miss by the upsurge of longing for a meeting with a twin soul.

When twin souls meet in incarnation, the danger is that the two beings may be over-absorbed in each other. This can directly affect the degree to which they move forward in their learning process and karmic redemption can be lessened. When partners are together, their range of experience is similar. By electing not to meet in incarnation, twin souls can cover as much complementary, evolutionary ground as possible.

It may be both disconcerting and disappointing to realise that we are unlikely to meet our perfect mate or other half in this present incarnation. Yet, once we know and understand this, a certain discontent and longing in us may be put to rest, as our expectations of the partner we *do* meet become more realistic. When this particular spiritual perspective is taken, we can see life as an evolutionary workplace and understand more about the overall organisation and intent behind the system in which we operate.

KARMIC THEMES AND TRIGGERS

In considering our choices of genetic family, soul family, body and gender a number of common karmic themes and triggers begin to emerge.

Negative themes and triggers are:

power;	opposition;
banishment;	neglect;
dependence/independence;	loneliness;
deprivation;	insecurity;
restriction;	repression;
loss of individuality;	abandonment;
exile;	loss;
rejection;	cruelty;
betrayal;	dislike/hatred.

Positive themes and triggers are:

empowerment;	co-operation;
inclusion;	nurturing;
sharing;	companionship;
abundance;	security;
kindness;	freedom;
blossoming;	confident individuality;
belonging;	welcome;
acquisition;	acceptance;
loyalty;	love.

As we identify potential karmic themes, so we begin to understand more of our greater selves. We also gain clues as to the
past scenarios in which we may have been involved and the
polarities and balances we are in this life to experience and
bring about. When we recognise polarity we can envision
balance. A case study will help as an illustration here.

Case Study: Laurence

Laurence came from a close, warm family. They were not
wealthy, but there was always enough, and his parents
provided security, nurturing, close lovingness and affection.
They liked celebrating family occasions with an abundance
of food, music and laughter.

Laurence had a talent for writing. His family encouraged him and wished he would share more of what he wrote
with them. Almost imperceptibly, at first, but more markedly
as time passed, Laurence seemed to withdraw from his
outgoing family, their warmth and their generous celebrations. When he left school he got a job as a reporter for a
local paper. His salary was quite meagre, but he insisted on
moving out from home into a shared house. There, he kept
himself to himself and began to take great pleasure in living
sparingly, to the point of self-denial. He became interested
not only in writing, but also in calligraphy. In the evenings
and at weekends he would shut himself away in his room
and practise the arts of writing beautifully.

The friends with whom he shared the house were toler-
ant of him and left him to lead his own life but his parents
became worried when one of these friends spoke of Laurence
as being an 'oddball'. They realised that their son, apart from
his outgoing job, was becoming withdrawn and too much of
a loner. Gradually, Laurence himself realised that his life was

out of balance and agreed to seek help from a counsellor, who, after a few sessions, suggested that he should come and have a session with me, since Laurence described himself as being in a spiritual, as well as a psychological, crisis.

He told me that he felt driven to withdraw. He sometimes found himself referring to his room as his 'cell'. He felt constrained to live frugally. Part of him loved the social aspect of his work as a reporter. He was genuinely interested in human stories and was beginning to be respected by his employers, but he felt this side of him to be in polarity with his other side.

Laurence was interested in spirituality and alternative approaches to religion. He had read about karma and reincarnation, and had dreams and visions of being a monk, in another time and place, in a strict, silent, religious order. This monk made frequent fasts and spent his days in prayer, contemplation and copying and illuminating manuscripts.

Secretly, Laurence had been wondering if he was going mad, because he had a sense that the monk of his dreams and visions was trying to take over his life and that this was making him powerless and compulsive.

Had Laurence actually been such a monk in another lifetime? It is both impossible and unnecessary to know. I did suggest, though, that Laurence was in the grip of a karmic polarity. He had chosen to be born into a family where there was an atmosphere of earthiness and sensuality. He had been attracted to work involving the research of stories of human interest and where he constantly needed to be present at human celebrations or moments of loss and tragedy. Part of him loved this and part of him was in rebellion against it. The obvious pathway forward was to find balance so that neither side of his personality gained ascendancy over the other.

Laurence needed continuing help from his counsellor. His case history illustrates the way in which psychological *and* spiritual growth need to go hand in hand. Laurence was better able to come to terms with his psychological problems, when his instinct that there was also a spiritual imbalance was accepted and supported. On the other hand, citing *only* karma as the source of his problems might have caused Laurence to slip too easily into 'victim' mode, with the danger of losing the power and motivation to get his life back on course. He is now well on the way to finding psychological *and* karmic balance. He knows that being caught between polarities can be a very painful experience until the journey to integration is made more conscious and the immediate power of the will is harnessed in the interests of balance.

EVOLUTIONARY CHALLENGES AND RE-PRESENTATIONS

Because of higher self choices, life presents us with karmic and evolutionary challenges. Until we make some sort of sense of these and bring them into awareness, they will continue to dog us or be re-presented to us. These re-presentations may be direct, challenging and confronting, simply telling us that we have not yet dealt with an issue. They may be knocks on the head or kicks from behind designed to shock us into awareness. They may be more subtle and not direct re-presentations at all. I often deal with people who are distressed because they feel as though they are going round in circles, meeting the same issues over and over again, making no progress or headway. Spiritual development has a spiralling motion. From time to time we pass over similar ground but the issues are revisited from a different perspective, as the spiral takes us both deeper and higher.

Before moving on to the next chapter, which looks at different kinds of karma, their implications and consequences, try the following exercises. Exercise 5 is designed to help with identifying personal karmic themes by looking at the polarities you may be experiencing in life. Exercise 6 considers the energies to be harnessed in order to get off the treadmill of retributive/repentant karma.

Exercise 5: Identifying Karmic Themes Represented by Life's Polarities and Frustrations

Before you begin this exercise you might like to look back at your life review from Exercise 1, page 22.

1. Take a large piece of paper and write down and underline the following headings at intervals down the page:

Too much
Too little
Exaggerated
Understated
Frustrations
Gratifications
Knocks on the head
Kicks from behind

2. Begin to consider these headings as they apply to your life. Use each heading as a question: 'What has been too much in my life?' 'What has been too little?' 'What has been exaggerated in my life?' 'What has been understated?' etc.

Also, where possible, turn the questions round to ask yourself: 'What would I like less of, from this moment forward?' 'What would I like more of, from this moment forward?'

3. When you come to 'Knocks on the head' and 'Kicks from behind', ask yourself: 'What did I learn from these?' 'How did they come about?' 'Was some individual in my life my teacher at such times – or was my teacher life itself?'

Try to allow yourself to 'free associate' around the questions, writing down all the thoughts that come, without stopping at this point to judge or evaluate them. Write down as many responses to each question as possible.

After about half-an-hour do the following:

4. Begin to look at what you have written. Which areas of your life have been your main focus? They may range from money to friends, from power to weakness, from sickness to health, from abundance to scarcity, from invasion to being unseen, from privilege to deprivation – and many more.

5. Ask yourself which, of the themes you have written down, seem as though they could represent polarities or over-compensations from another lifetime. For instance, if you always have to struggle to be seen or heard in your present lifetime, maybe you could surmise that you might have been over-pushy before – or maybe you neglected to see or hear the needs of others in some way.

6. Choose, for consideration, one of the themes or polarities you have identified. Realise that at the higher level your higher self has chosen to give you this experience in this lifetime. Close your eyes and try to visualise the sort of person, scenario or behaviour that might have prompted your higher self to make this choice, this time around.

Exercise 6: Getting Off the Treadmill

One of the pitfalls of a belief in karma is that it can make us feel victims of circumstance. As well as experience, other main goals of evolution are consciousness and self-responsibility. It is important to remember that we can live creatively, even if certain restrictions operate in our lives. This is a meditative guided visualisation, to help in gathering your inner resources to make changes in your life.

Making sure that you will be undisturbed, sit or lie in a comfortable, but symmetrically balanced position. Have a blanket for warmth, as well as crayons, paper and pencils on hand for any drawing or recording you may wish to do.

Become aware of the rhythm of your breathing. Feel each in-breath and each out-breath. Do not try to breathe in a particular way; just let your breath grow steady and find its own natural, relaxed level.

Enter your inner space and imagine that you can hear running and rhythmically churning water. Walk along an inner pathway until you come to a beautiful scene where swiftly flowing water is turning a mill wheel. You know that the mill wheel, powered by the water, is, in turn, powering machinery, perhaps for grinding purposes. There is a sense of agelessness and continuity about this scene.

Nearby, there is a meadow, where you can lie in soft, longish grass, in the sun. The fragrance of natural flowers is around you, you can hear a soft wind in the trees, birds singing and maybe bees humming as they visit flowers, collecting nectar. You can still hear the water and the pulsing of the mill wheel. You may reflect that in bygone days animals or slaves were sometimes used to turn mills. Endlessly treading, to keep the wheels turning. Animals and slaves were often chained into position on such wheels, required to work and keep up a rhythm beyond the bounds of normal stamina.

Now, only a few water wheels and some windmills remain, but the memory of 'treadmills' lives on in our language. We speak, symbolically, of any overworn routine as 'a treadmill'. Is there a treadmill situation in your outer life or inner belief? Are you metaphorically chained to old rhythms and patterns? Do you feel yourself to be 'a victim of circumstance'? As you lie in the meadow, hearing natural sounds and the churn of the water wheel, realise that we are not truly tied to our symbolic treadmills. There are no real chains or bonds. We are free to step off, walk away and find 'pastures new'. There are creative opportunities. Our higher selves do not expect unmitigating sacrifices for past causes. There may be some limitations, but there is always enough leeway to find the way to make our hearts sing.

When you are ready, walk back once more to where you can see the watermill. It is turned by a natural force, not by forced labour. Remember this and your potential freedom from all symbolic bondage as you become aware once again of the rhythm of your breathing and the contact of your body with chair or floor. Come fully into the present and ground yourself and your inner meditative experiences by drawing or writing, peacefully, for a while.

Chapter 5
THE KARMIC ARRAY

This is its work upon the things you see,
The unseen things are more; men's hearts and minds,
The thoughts of peoples and their ways and wills,
Those, too, the great Law binds ...

BEYOND THE PERSONAL • KARMIC MECHANISMS • KARMIC
DEBT • KARMIC ENMESHMENT • KARMIC PARALYSIS •
INSTANT KARMA • FAMILY KARMA • GROUP KARMA •
SYNCHRONICITY • DRAMA AND DISASTER • GROUP KARMA
TODAY • YIN AND YANG • EXERCISE 7 KNOCKS ON THE HEAD
AND KICKS FROM BEHIND

BEYOND THE PERSONAL

As individuals in evolution it is difficult to avoid setting karmic causes into action. We cannot live effectively without making ripples on the pond. Spiritually and karmically we must be aware of personal responsibility. Yet, as incarnate beads or grains from a central soul thread or core, we are part of a complex journey. Souls have kin, belong to groups (see page 49), join each other in incarnation as races and nations and are all, ultimately, members of the great human family. Although we might have pre-incarnational agreements with others, similar to standing in the wings, writing a meaningful play to be enacted (see page 48), the karmic law of cause and effect might also be described as 'wheels within wheels'.

Beyond personal karma and evolution there is family karma, beyond family, there is group karma, beyond group there is racial or national karma, beyond race or nation, there is the karma of the whole of humanity. Surrounding these main streams of karma there are karmic mechanisms such as karmic debt and karmic enmeshment. There is even instant karma.

In this chapter, different aspects of this karmic array or spectrum are considered, including some individual stories.

KARMIC MECHANISMS

The three main stages of karmic outworking – retributive/penitent, redemptive and transcendent karma – have already been described in Chapter 3 (pages 56–8). As well as karmic stages there are other common karmic states or mechanisms. These can operate powerfully with the forces of synchronicity. Sometimes we find ourselves in situations where everything seems highlighted or perhaps brings us that 'larger than life' feeling. We may feel tied to a certain situation or person by bonds that are beyond our control, or wish, to sever.

KARMIC DEBT

People who come for spiritual guidance often say, of a particular situation or relationship, such things as 'I know I am giving almost too much – but it seems right'; 'I seem to be tied to this situation, but part of me does not want to be free';

'There is no logical explanation as to why I should feel indebted to A, but I am'.

Current life psychological factors must always be given priority and cleared, before wider aspects such as past lives and karma are considered. But often the feelings and experiences come from beyond psychological bondage. Examining the possibility of karmic debt is often a relief, permission or release.

In the broadest sense karmic debts are the effects we have set in motion by previous behaviour. They can be seen in relationship to our personal evolution, to society or to other individuals. If, in order to balance out a life of licentiousness, I choose to become a nun in a subsequent life, I am repaying a debt to myself and, in part, to society. If I follow up a lifetime as a corrupt administrator by becoming a philanthropist I am paying a debt to society. At the more personal level karmic debts are acquired when we fail in our duty to others, but also when others go beyond the call of duty in order to help us in a particularly difficult situation.

Case Study: Karen

In psychological terms Karen could be seen as being over-protective to her daughter, Denise, who, at over thirty, was still afraid of life and independence. Denise still lived at home and had always done so. She had studied at university, but in her home town and with no desire, it seemed, to join in the regular student experience of hostel or flat share. After university Denise had taken an undemanding, low-paid job, far below her intellectual potential.

Karen was a single parent and friends and family had criticised her for 'making a rod for her own back', accused her of limiting Denise's opportunities and failing to require her to be satisfactorily independent or self-sufficient.

Both Karen and Denise had seen psychological and emotional dangers in their situation and had, separately and together, been for counselling to look at all the possibilities of over-compensation, co-dependency and escapism. They had admitted that such factors existed in their relationship and life situation. They had worked on themselves accordingly. But it was not enough.

Karen came to me, seeking a wider spiritual view. As she considered the possibilities offered by past lives and karma she began to feel strongly that she owed Denise a karmic debt. She had always had dreams of a particular neglected child, which persisted even after she learned to nurture her own inner child and in spite of the fact that she had certainly never neglected Denise. She said:

> 'I have always felt that I am working something out with Denise, but have been thrown into doubt by the criticism of others and by the possible psychological factors. I have even feared that our relationship might be emotionally incestuous. When I consider karmic debt as an explanation, then I feel that all I/we need to do is go on playing this situation by ear and do our best to be impervious to the criticism of others.'

With occasional need for reassurance and clarity, over the next two years Karen continued her support for, and protection of, Denise. At a certain point things began to change. Denise became more sociable, discovered her sexuality and began to enjoy relating to men and to life in general. She undertook some further professional training and eventually moved away to a new job and a flat of her own. Now, five years on, she is planning to marry. Karen is delighted – but feels that had she not followed her intuition or instinct to nurture and provide until Denise moved on naturally, things might not have resolved themselves so successfully. She feels strongly that she had a karmic debt to Denise because of neglect of her in a previous life. She also believes that Denise allowed her to repay that karmic debt until the scales were balanced and both could move on. Karen's neglected child dreams have ceased.

THE DRUIDIC VIEW

Before moving on from karmic debt it is worth mentioning that records in the British Museum show that ancient Druids in the early first century AD believed so strongly in reincarnation that they were quite happy to arrange repayment of favours or debts for a future lifetime. They recognised that those who were impoverished in one life would probably be blessed in the next. Therefore, help from the fortunate for the unfortunate could be given with thought only of repayment in a future existence.

KARMIC ENMESHMENT

When fully understood and interpreted the karmic law of cause and effect makes us supremely responsible for all our actions and interactions in life. If we fail in our accountability towards others in one life, then we shall have to find some way of recompensing for that failure in a later life. In the case study above we saw that Karen believed she had previously failed in her parenting role to Denise. She instinctively knew that, in the present lifetime, neither she, nor her daughter, would be free to move on until the repayment of this karmic debt came to a natural resolution. Karen was happy to await this natural resolution, in course of time. She felt no resentment about Denise's needs and the limit they put on her own freedom. When Denise was ready to move on, Karen, once more, felt no resentment. She was able to enjoy the sense of fulfilment that comes when a task has reached a successful conclusion.

Others had suggested to Karen that she was being imprisoned or exploited by Denise. They were seeing something that she, personally, did not feel. The karmic picture might have been different *had* Karen felt confined and manipulated. If there had been other things Karen desperately wanted to do and then later blamed Denise for standing in the way of her being free to live her own life, then the mechanism of karmic enmeshment could have come into play. In over-paying one karmic debt, another could have been incurred. A subsequent situation might have come into being in which Denise had the task of setting Karen free.

When we are conscious of karmic cause and effect it is well to be both aware, and wary, of any resentments we build towards others in life. It is easy to 'blame' others for the risks we have failed to take or the opportunities we have missed. We make 'excuses' such as: 'Having mother to look after meant I could never travel'; or 'I didn't move to that better job in the North of England because of disrupting the children's schooling'; or 'My wife could not have coped with living abroad'. These can be karmic danger signals. We should only make those sacrifices for which we take full responsibility. To hold others culpable for the limitations we put on ourselves is to invite karmic enmeshment.

We are free of bondage only when we are able to make positive statements about limitations we have accepted: 'I've found it such a privilege to look after Mother that I decided to do it wholeheartedly. Giving up travel was a small price to pay'; 'If I'd moved to that job in the North of England everything might have changed – I was happy with a less glamorous post, focusing my attention on the family and the children's schooling'.

KARMIC PARALYSIS

Continuity of consciousness and evolution through many lifetimes means that when a personality bead or grain 'dies', or goes to the 'between life' state or plane, a life review has to be made (see pages 17–18). From the wider perspective of realms beyond the physical, the fuller implications of the ripples we have made on the pond of life or the sea of evolution are seen. During this review our fuller being may experience shock waves when the repercussions and outworkings of actions or omissions are seen. A fear of the consequences of our actions will be particularly registered where we have abused or misused any form of power, accountability to others or authority.

Fear of our own success is an obstacle many of us may recognise at some time in our lives. There may be psychological reasons for this. Yet we might also be suffering from a 'paralysis' due to the shock waves encountered during a higher level life review. Recognising that wise use of success or responsibility, rather than avoidance, will bring balance and further our spiritual evolution can be the spur that gives us the courage to break restrictive patterns.

INSTANT KARMA

In the wider scheme of things it is difficult to separate karma from reincarnation and many lifetimes (see also pages 8–11). Yet, of course, instant karma exists. We do not always have to await death and another incarnation in order to deal with the results of our actions. If we are aware enough and humble enough to see and balance our faults in the here and now, then the karmic burden to be sorted out in any future life becomes much lighter. We can learn much from the 'Mrs Do-As-You-Would-Be-Done-By' philosophy immortalised by Charles Kingsley in *Tom and the Water Babies*.

In some respects, where true justice operates in the legal systems of society, we can appreciate the immediate value of our incarnate regard for the archetype of justice. Good laws might be seen as instruments in ensuring that certain effects of actions or causes set in motion are instantly purged. Reasonable law and order can be the vehicle for redress of instant karma. Respect for legality can prevent us from taking actions we might later regret. Law systems based on over-punishment or brutality could be a cause of group or national karma (see page 97).

As we evolve our lives become more congruent until we transcend the polarities of life. Our pendulum no longer swings to extremes. Ultimately, we take no unfinished business with us to other realms and so move beyond the need for mortal incarnation.

FAMILY KARMA

Family karma can manifest in the form of an inherited genetic trait or illness, an incomplete family task or family pride. It becomes family, rather than personal karma, when several members of the family share the restrictions, limitations, sense of purpose or joint task. An obvious example on the, perhaps, more positive side, is that of inherited wealth. Guardianship of wealth, beautiful things or large amounts of land can be a joint family task with considerable spiritual implications and with many pitfalls for the unwary.

Leadership, or more often rulership, can also denote a family karmic or evolutionary task. Monarchs and their offspring are often locked into a destiny, which though it may seem to bring many privileges, can also be narrow and demanding.

Case Study: Arnold

Arnold was the oldest son in a family of land-owning farmers. Large stretches of the arable and pasture land around the English rural village in which he lived had belonged to his family for generations. It was expected that all family members, male and female, would take up farming and country pursuits as their career. Whenever an oldest, married son celebrated the arrival of his first child it was expected that he would move in to the main farmhouse. The new grandparents would then move into one of the other properties owned by the extended family.

Arnold was not a happy farmer. Instead of looking forward to the moment when he would move into the beautiful, old farmhouse, he dreaded it. He looked forward to the birth of his first child with mixed feelings. Family pressure and tradition was such that he did not feel able to express how he felt or to confide, even to his wife, what his true feelings and secret ambitions were. His wife, Lucy, also came from a farming family. Some of her expectations of marriage with Arnold were bound up in the tradition of the family into which she had married. She enjoyed moving into the farmhouse and set about putting her own stamp upon it. These alterations and modernisations were funded from the family business and regarded as part of the rite of passage bound up in this tradition.

Arnold farmed on, playing the role expected of him. He was a competent farmer. Two more children were born. To all outer appearances the family tradition was continuing satisfactorily and without interruption. The landowner destiny and karmic inheritance were being fulfilled. Yet, as has been noted before, one of the main functions of karma is to bring about consciousness in living.

A karmic inheritance may best fulfil its purpose when it leads an individual or group of individuals to *question* destiny. In the case of Arnold's family, generations had unquestioningly tilled the soil, harvested the crops and husbanded the animals. We can only speculate as to the original acquisition of land by Arnold's distant ancestors. It could have come from a will to power, from vision about proper management of food provision, from a sense of service to others, or from a karmic drive to be more in touch with the earth. To Arnold's more immediate ancestors and extended family, if they ever thought about it, it was a privilege and a natural progression. These family members accepted farming, almost unthinkingly, as their birthright. Perhaps this is why the pattern had to change, with Arnold as the catalyst.

Hidden stress and lack of support can provoke a health crisis. The body often tells us when enough is enough. Arnold was suddenly rushed to hospital with a perforated stomach ulcer.

The resources of the extended family carried the crisis efficiently. Lucy, Arnold and their children had all the support and practical help they could need. The farming wheels continued to turn smoothly, even though, normally, Arnold was a main cog in their works. To aid his convalescence Arnold and Lucy were encouraged to take a holiday alone, without their children.

After the worst of his illness crisis, Arnold had quietly been observing the results of his absence and had been reminded of the family strengths, which always rallied in the interests of their long traditional dedication to the land. During his time away with Lucy, he was finally able to speak of his unhappiness with his destiny and his ambitions for change. He had long had secret dreams of opening a high-class country restaurant. He even knew the exact barn, on the family land, near to easy access, which could be successfully converted to house such a venture. Contrary to his expectations, Lucy was supportive, and even excited, about the appearance of this new facet in her husband.

There were long family conferences ahead. The wealth of land-owning families is literally in the soil they farm. Raising capital and breaking with tradition was not easy. There were storms and recriminations, but eventually Arnold, with Lucy's support, won through. The family supported his venture, weathered the change and the new generation now has choice – the farming side of the business or the restaurant. Hopefully any over-bearing weight of traditional expectation has also been lifted from younger family members. Arnold broke the mould and set a precedent for others to do the same, should they so wish.

Arnold's story was revealed in a workshop, when he and Lucy became interested in personal and spiritual growth. Arnold felt that he had been born into that family tradition for two main reasons. He had a sense that in his past he had denied others opportunity to develop their true gifts. Choosing to be born into an entrenched family tradition had then, for him, been retributive/penitent karma. He also felt that the family needed a catalyst for the specific purpose of breaking the mould of complacency. He did not feel like a cuckoo in the nest. There had been some consternation when his ambition had been revealed, but the family had been supportive and, if anything, had become closer because of what had happened. He felt his family to be spiritual rather than genetic and that they had successfully staged and enacted together a pre-planned karmic drama.

GROUP KARMA

Family karma, as illustrated by the case study of Arnold above, is, in its own sense, group karma. Yet there are wider instances of group karma being enacted all around us. If we reflect on the many ramifications of why we choose our family of birth then we must also reflect on the unseen forces, which, later in life, connect us with wider experiences. Each city, town, village or neighbourhood street, to which we are drawn, can represent opportunities for karmic learning. Perspectives may be subtly different, but the experience of a life lived out mainly in London is quite different from life in the wilds of Yorkshire or the Outer Hebrides. Different opportunities, different obstacles, different dangers requiring the harnessing of different resources apply according to geographic location. Even neighbouring towns and villages in a smaller area have different characteristics inherited and perpetuated by the nature of the groups of people who gather in them.

Beyond our families, and in addition to the communities in which we live, we join or become affiliated with groups wielding different degrees of influence within national or human life. Often, by the nature or requirement of our work, we become members of a group or a group within a group. Each school has a group of teachers, those teachers belong to the national teaching body and maybe to professional sub-groups within that body. Our workplace is usually a group place, the nature of our work unites us with others working with similar skills or to similar purpose. We experience our work individually and subjectively but also communally. We join unions or professional organisations and so link our personal experience with wider experience in co-operation or interdependency. As practitioners of a skill, providers of a service, members of a trade or profession, we belong energetically to an operative force-field. As part of that field and the contribution we bring to it, we encounter further areas in which to work with retributive/repentant, redemptive and transcendent karma, not only at a personal but at a group level. The groups of which we are a part have a karmic inheritance of causes set in motion by former members of such groups. Future generations will reap the benefits of our contributions or the effects of the causes, both negative and positive, which we set in motion.

Our individual karmic and evolutionary experience requirements will play a major part in determining which group we join. Our specific energies will help to shape the group; the group energy will play its part in shaping us. Different groups engage with different archetypes. Our growth and expansion is played out in a series of interconnecting, interacting arenas, where we reap what others have sown and sow what others will reap. Fashion and trends, actions and reactions, in our work and community lives, play their part in presenting and re-presenting the polarity swings that eventually bring about balance for ourselves as individuals and for society as a whole.

A PERSONAL EXAMPLE

Part of my working experience has been as a teacher. I count myself lucky that a large part of my teaching experience happened during the expansive 1960s in a county with a forward-looking attitude to education. I did not love teaching, yet in the primary schools of that area, at that time, there was a sense of dedication and excitement. Children learned through informal methods. They learned well. They reached high standards. As classroom teachers we had a high level of support from advisers and enlightened inspectors.

Towards the end of my time as a teacher, economic cutbacks were occurring and a reaction to open-plan classrooms, activity based and integrated day teaching methods had set in. Undoubtedly, in some areas the pendulum swing to informality in teaching had swung too far. Today those methods are largely blamed for a lowering of educational standards in the UK. But is the swing to more formal methods and rigorous testing going too far? The teachers of today are reaping the effects of some of the causes set in motion by those 'feel-good' years. Hopefully, a healthy balance will eventually emerge, but if the pendulum swings too far in an opposite direction, teachers and pupils alike will be caught in a chain reaction. The teaching profession is working out some group karma. The 'knock-on' effects are tremendous. They affect us all. Several individual, group and universal karmic themes could be highlighted, but issues of power and establishment, rigidity and flexibility, order and chaos are certainly to the fore.

SYNCHRONICITY

The simultaneous occurrence of events, appearing to be meaningfully related without apparent causal connection, has held a long fascination for thinkers, psychologists and philosophers. Synchronicity, in spiritual philosophy, is seen as operating in order to bring about opportunity and awareness. The forces drawing us towards each other, for various purposes to be fulfilled, are synchronous forces. They may be particularly operative in alerting us to group tasks or group karma. If our souls are intent on a meeting, it will manifest in one way or another.

Some years ago, six people unknown to each other at the time but who later discovered that they had a meaningful healing project to fulfil together, went to a large, four-hundred-strong conference. Though by their mutual attendance at this event their paths had, to some extent, crossed, they did not make direct contact with each other. Three years later, each one of these individuals attended a small conference of twelve people where contact and the recognition of their joint project could not be avoided. When they realised that they *might* have met on that previous occasion, they experienced a sense of awe. Their subsequent working together became especially meaningful and they each felt that the forces of synchronicity had insistently brought them together so that they could complete a task and resolve karmically unfinished business.

DRAMA AND DISASTER

When communities, nations or humanity itself are involved in drama and disaster, such as the tragedies of Aberfan, Lockerbie, Hungerford and Dunblane, in the UK, or Turkish earthquakes, Ethiopian famine and the shooting at Columbine High in the US, we might ask whether some thread of destiny has drawn particular people together in order to share or to play particular roles in a big and shocking experience. The ramifications are always great. In overcoming danger, pain, suffering and loss we often see examples of tremendous courage and heroism. In these times of sophisticated communications, whole nations, even the whole world, share the shock waves and something of the horror. A drama is enacted with repercussions for the group immediately involved, the individuals within that group, a nation and perhaps even the whole of humanity.

Such happenings, if they are to be seen in the light of karma, require us to go beyond the over-simplistic 'eye for an eye and tooth for a tooth', 'as ye sow so shall ye reap', definitions of the law of cause and effect. Even though each individual's experience within a group calamity will have personal definition, we cannot draw the conclusion that everyone involved has 'brought this on' through personal cause and effect. Neither can we, economically (in the philosophical sense), conclude that this group, as a group, did something together in a past life which necessitated the outworking they are now experiencing in present times. Instead, we must focus more on karma as an evolutionary tool. At this level, it is not only about individual evolution but about the spiritual maturation of the human race as a whole. Each individual in conscious spiritual growth contributes to this, mainly by coming to terms with the range of archetypal forces constantly influencing and shaping our lives (see page 29).

As we have seen (on page 78), individuals are spurred into spiritual consciousness by the obstacles and/or blessings – chosen from the higher self level – to accompany their incarnate lives. Yet, although the individual cell must affect the whole of the body of humanity, mass awakening needs higher profile prompts.

My spiritual teacher (see Glossary) is not alone in suggesting that humanity is on the brink of a new and golden age. Since the dawn of human life we have been following a path of knowledge and experience, which, when finally assimilated, will put us into an ultimate position of choice, linked to a true understanding of Divine Will and Purpose. At this point, the negative or shadow archetypes will no longer have power over us, since, through our knowledge of their destructiveness, we shall eventually deny them life force.

Whenever disasters erupt, shadow archetypes have taken centre-stage. In overcoming them and minimising their devastating effects, qualities of true humanity and human community are called into play. Measures to prevent repeats or re-presentations are put into motion. The vision of a better quality of life for humanity receives serious attention. Our contract to fellow members of the human race becomes clearer. We attempt to diagnose what is out of balance, unite against the invasion of disruptive forces and help each other to find a way through. Thus, the individual experience reflects into group experience which, in turn, mirrors into national experience and thence enters total human awareness. Coping with disaster can empower us to eradicate destructiveness and promote positive change.

Just as Arnold became a catalyst for change in a family situation, as we saw in the case study above, so groups dealing with opposition change nations, and nations change the whole. All nations and races carry distinguishing characteristics, and most have debts to humanity caused by anti-humanitarian behaviour. For example, war-mongering, ethnic cleansing, over-colonisation, religious, racial or political intolerance and the drive for power can usually be given national labels or be racially attributed. The karmic causes, which distinct large groups, races or nations set in motion, affect us all. We all bear the effects of war, invasion, mass exile and opposition suffered by our fellow humans but as we do so, we perhaps learn to work for peace, tolerance and mutual respect. This is particularly evident now, where the television screens in our homes are literally a window on the world, showing us what is happening, as it is happening, and awakening humanitarian consciousness perhaps as never before.

GROUP KARMA TODAY

When, before incarnation, our higher selves select the historical time and culture for our entry or re-entry into the world, the opportunity for service to a particular group, or in the interests of group change, is often taken into account. Pendulum swings at the collective level have to be redressed just as urgently as at the personal level. These swings are one of the mechanisms of karma with the main purpose of leading us, eventually, to balance, wisdom and oneness with the Source.

Using the word God to describe the Creative Source within the universe is, in the West, a difficult mode to avoid. It implies, and has become associated with, the elevation of the masculine principle as a supreme force. In the current atmosphere of equal opportunities this can be seen as politically incorrect. But, at a far deeper level, it is philosophically incorrect. Creativity is the product of an interaction between the masculine and feminine principles. Giving God a Goddess as a wife, or introducing, as some churches do, references to the Father/Mother God, is unsatisfactory. Such practices border on the anthropomorphic, and are, at the same time, over-simplistic and tautological. The source of all that *is*, has to be the unseen place or timeless moment where there is such an integral, balanced interaction between masculine and feminine principles, that the miracle of the universe remains constantly in manifestation.

YIN AND YANG

If a major aspect of karmic evolution is learning to balance polarities, then the yin/yang polarities are probably the most vital and powerful of the forces that require equilibrium. (The principles of yin and yang are described on page 69.) Because the original spark of the soul splits into yin and yang for purposes of evolution, it is inevitable that the two principles become polarised in the journey of life. Male and female battle for equality, but yin and yang nestle together, accepting their difference and recognising that there is no wholeness, life force, creativity or completion *unless* they are so nestled.

It seems likely that humanity is on the brink of a great spiritual and evolutionary breakthrough. It can be that our present times are so troubled with violence and war *because* we are finally ready to resolve or transcend some major polarities. We have to see and experience them, in full consciousness, before we can resolve them. In the West we are seeing, also, a major outworking between the sexes. Roughly half the population is male and half, female – the two major, vital and basic groups of humanity. Of course women carry more yin, and men more yang energy, but both have the seed of the other within them. Women use the masculine principle for some functions and men use the feminine. Men and women are different – but they are as necessary to each other, and as equal in that necessity, as is yin to yang in the true whole.

In present times – certainly in the Western world – to be a man or to be a woman is to be part of a renegotiation of the gender roles. In this task we need to hold the yin/yang vision in consciousness, so that the search for equality of opportunity does not become a battle for superiority, with the pendulum swinging strongly in full arc and the polarities holding us trapped.

We achieve full evolution when we re-merge with the Source. The work of manifesting a society in which yin and yang nestle happily and naturally together in the circle of completion, celebrating their difference as the source of creativity, is a gender-related, group karma task.

Exercise 7: Knocks on the Head and Kicks from Behind - Relating More Positively to Obstacles and Causes in Life

This is a contemplative exercise. You will need to look again at the work you did on Exercise 1 (page 22). You will need to have worked through Exercise 1 before this present exercise can be meaningful.

Look at your notes and drawings from Exercise 1. Look particularly at:

- the obstacles you have encountered in your life
- any illnesses you have had
- any accidents that have happened to you
- losses you have endured
- frustrations of will or choice from whichever direction or in whatever way these may have happened.

Be aware of any resentment, grudge or anger you bear towards others, life, circumstances, authority – perhaps to 'God' or your own higher self.

Read through again and contemplate the sections of this chapter sub-headed: Karmic enmeshment, Karmic paralysis and Instant karma.

On one sheet of paper write down some sentences that express your frustrations and resentments (e.g. 'If only my parents had not pressurised me into taking that job in the bank I might have gone to art school').

Try to see and express honestly any negativity you feel around each of the obstacles you have identified.

Take a second sheet of paper and maybe a different coloured pen and write down some sentences that turn your initial perceptions around or bring out some positive element in them (e.g. 'If I hadn't worked in that bank I would never have met the person I now love, have married and so brought the children we have into the world'; 'If I hadn't worked in that bank I would never have learned discipline and money management'; 'If I hadn't worked in that bank I would never have known just how strongly I needed to study art – it feels good to have taken my own responsibility for changing direction' and so on).

If you feel that you are still tending to 'blame' any person or circumstance in your life for preventing you from having access to opportunity, ask yourself why you still allow yourself to be in bondage to the past or to others. What are the fears/old patterns/lack of permission preventing you from moving on? Is there something you could change? Could you create a new sense of direction in your life by seeing more things as positive pointers to enabling you to know what you really want from the future?

What positive life skills have you developed from your experiences of adversity?

You may need to come back to this exercise on more than one occasion. Your aim is to see the areas of life into which you can bring some positive creativity and find a sense of non-punitive meaning in the challenges life has given you.

Chapter 6
LIVING
SOULFULLY

It will not be contemned of anyone;
Who thwarts it loses, and who serves it gains;
The hidden good it pays with peace and bliss,
The hidden ill with pains ...

AKASHIC RECORDS

One of the main aims of this book has been to show the wise, compassionate, positive and free-choice aspects of the karmic law of cause and effect in order to dispel ideas that it is a punitive, imposed, judgemental and limiting structure. Karma, as a law, ensures that we evolve. Record keeping is an inbuilt facet of its outworkings and mechanisms. The central consciousness of the soul thread or core assimilates the totality of incarnational experience and assesses progress. It makes decisions and choices, relating to benefits accrued, experience still required and imbalances to be redressed. In the tradition of karma, there is also implication of a complex overall imprint of the total experience of the human race throughout its history and evolution. This imprint is known by the Sanskrit word: *'akasha'*. The akashic records carry the chronicles of individual and collective actions from the first moment of the dawning of human consciousness.

Though most of us do not consciously recall other lifetimes (see also page 63), we carry their influence unconsciously. The imprint of the akashic records is all around us. Some people actively train themselves to read these records, while others claim to be able to read them on behalf of others. As we saw in Chapter 1, Joan Grant wrote several books about her own past-life recalls, presenting them mostly as novels. Later she found that she could access the past lives of others. Eventually she worked with the psychiatrist Denys Kelsey and together they helped many people to find the source of behaviour problems or neuroses and so to release them, often quite miraculously (see Bibliography).

THE COLLECTIVE UNCONSCIOUS

The psychologist C. G. Jung (see Bibliography) perceived something similar to akashic records in his writings about the 'collective unconscious'. Nothing experienced or learned by human beings, individually, or collectively, is ever lost. It may go dormant for a while, but as we add to our skills and make discoveries we never start entirely from scratch. It is not only that we are able to *study* former progress in any area of research or intended breakthrough, but that, unconsciously, we attune to what has gone before. There is a memory bank to which we have intuitive and instinctual access. Further than this, our immediate thoughts and experiences affect everyone around us, in the moment, far more than we commonly suppose to be possible. Our individual energy fields are interactive, sensitive and porous. 'No man is an island' has been well said.

It is not only those who know themselves to be 'psychic' who are energetically and subtly affected by mass triumphs or disasters *before* hearing details of them. Many of us experience an unexplained feeling of uplift or of impending doom and depression, unrelated to immediate personal circumstances, preceding good or bad local, national or international news. Bank holidays, days which the French call '*jours des fêtes*', even weekends, have a different atmosphere from ordinary working days and, subliminally, we all pick up on this.

MORPHIC RESONANCE

Rupert Sheldrake (see Bibliography) writes of 'morphic resonance' or the 'hundredth monkey theory', explaining that when an optimum number of a species is taught a new behaviour, then all the members of that species will change a pattern without actively having learned it. Thus, if one monkey on an island learns to wash potatoes and teaches another, who teaches another, when an optimum number of monkeys on the island wash potatoes then the whole of the monkey species everywhere will begin to wash potatoes. British blue tits originally taught each other to open foil-topped milk bottles delivered to doorsteps – now all blue tits know, without consciously learning, how to open milk bottles on doorsteps! This sort of learning is not confined to animals. Jung (psychologist), Eliot (philosophic poet) and

Toynbee (historian) are well-known voices among those who have spoken about a 'creative minority' or 'critical mass' for humanity. When an optimum number of people make positive changes in their behaviour, then the whole of humanity will automatically make those changes too. Mass vigils, world days of prayer and 'two-minute silences' all work subtly, as well as obviously, to raise the consciousness of the whole.

Great discoveries, such as the invention of the wheel, happen by simultaneous revelation rather than in one place, with the information being passed on by word of mouth or demonstration. In more recent times, when separate investigative teams, working independently or in different parts of the world, have come concurrently to a research breakthrough, there have been bitter suspicions, accusations and counter-accusations concerning possible leakage or espionage. Usually, such mistrust is unfounded. The coincidence of breakthrough is another demonstration of our facility for unconscious, but synchronous, interaction.

POSITIVE KARMA

As this present book suggests, by taking the wider view of karma and tracing patterns in our lives, we can find structure, purpose, meaning and explanation for living. We can do this mentally, by deduction, or imaginatively and intuitively as suggested and guided in the exercises given. We do not have to know or be able to relive our past lives categorically, in order to appreciate the probable wider ramifications of the karmic law of cause and effect. If we can get insight into our battle with the polarities (see also pages 70–4), imaginatively reconstruct the causes we have created by omission and commission, acknowledge that the karmic laws are not only about sin but also about evolution, then we can also appreciate an even more positive aspect of karma. We can, as the title of this chapter states, live soulfully. This means that we can become more conscious of the positive learning acquired by our souls, during the course of their evolution.

The beads on our soul thread or grains on our soul core have accumulated a great deal of life experience. Our personal akashic records carry the imprint of skills, training, philosophising, knowledge and understanding. As discussed in pages 62–4, in the interest of the new experiences required for evolution, we may be blocked from revisiting old ground, but we do not always have to start from scratch in learning the skills of life. Most people have some area of giftedness, talent or natural aptitude. Some, but by no means all, of these are imparted by genetic inheritance. When we are more aware of ourselves we might often say: 'It does not feel new'; 'it is as though I have done this before'; 'I seem to know more than I actually learn or am taught'; 'I am a natural-born dancer, writer, linguist, musician, artist, healer, teacher …'.

GIFTEDNESS

With our tendency to see life and spiritual development as a hard, demanding slog, we can be poor channels for joy and celebration – particularly of ourselves. Naming some of the talents and aptitudes we have as 'gifts' is so semantically common that we perhaps do not entirely appreciate what a truth this is. Talented and gifted people may, in one sense, be especially favoured. Yet the gifts of great artists, musicians, writers, actors, creators, discoverers, healers, teachers and leaders reach out to and inspire us all. The possession of a talent may come from personal positive karma or it may be plucked from collective, cumulative experience, but we all receive and benefit from its effects as part of a common but rich inheritance. If we focus too much on the retributive/repentant aspects of karma, the positive way in which karmic effect can also bring us benefits, rewards and bounty to lighten our existence, can go unacknowledged. The karmic causes of learning, study and practice have the karmic effects of producing expertise and enabling the blossoming of genius. Though we do not remember previous lifetimes consciously, we do not always have to start at the novice or apprentice stage with everything as lifetime follows lifetime.

KARMIC REWARD

The use of the term 'reward' is not intended to re-evoke the narrow interpretation of karma as a law of punishment and recompense, but to emphasise that positive gains go alongside all the mechanisms of polarity and balance. No third party doles out unpleasant tasks or obstacles and neither are there any rewarding trophies – but cumulative effort does bring its own rewards. Not all our choices for any given lifetime will be concerned with difficulties and obstacles – we also choose to bring skills to offer to others and to have at least some spiritually compatible life companions. We reward ourselves, and when we view life from a constructive perspective and focus on spiritual and symbolic blessings, as well as material good fortune, the areas in which we are favoured become ever clearer. The ability to appreciate that we are always in the right place at the right time is a vital ingredient in living magically. It is also a sign that we are getting the hang of karma, reaping the rewards of experience and overcoming any victim consciousness.

TALENTS IN THE BANK

It is important to discover and develop our special gifts, but the talents and aptitudes that we have can often lie dormant. The expectations or requirements of society, the vision of parents for their children, and the training and opportunities they see as leading to our ultimate well-being are the cause of a collusive moulding process (see also page 71). Children *want* to fit in and have approval. Due to familial and social conditioning, latent talents can stay dormant until we are well into adulthood or even later in life. We may be well into, or even past, middle age before we experience that malaise, so aptly described by C. G. Jung, as 'a discontent with being normal'.

Of course, our karmic process may *require* late development and self-discovery in order for us to meet the obstacles of retributive/repentant karma. But those obstacles also serve to make us more conscious about, and responsible for, our pathway to fulfilment. When we are aware enough, within ourselves, to take steps to overcome our stumbling blocks, then energies such as synchronicity usually flow with us to a remarkable degree, aiding the important transition to redemptive karma (see also page 57).

Finding the courage to 'go off at a tangent' from expectations heaped upon us, or to leave behind earlier training and career direction, is not easy, but the treading of our karmic path, the growth of our psyches and souls and our physical health and well-being may depend upon it.

Discovering a latent or repressed gift, talent or expertise, later in life, can be exciting – but scary. The realisation that you are a potter, social worker, healer, writer, bridge-builder, etc., *manqué*, can represent a real crossroad point in life and tax one's creative decision making or life planning to the full. Heavy responsibilities to others are often acquired along life's way. Honouring self *and* duty, when life changes call, can be a challenge to the point of crisis. Self-sacrifice, without clarity, can be both psychologically and karmically complicated (see Karmic enmeshment, page 90), even though allowing and accepting sacrifice from others during a transition period can be a part of the learning process for all concerned.

Once the talent has been recognised and the decision made to allow it expression, the speed with which mastery comes will often be astonishing. Such skills have not only lain dormant for a considerable period in the present lifetime, but have been carried in soul memory for, perhaps, many aeons. The karmic reasons for their re-emergence range from group to personal karmic planning. Maybe society or a section of society with which the talented individual has contact needs that gift now – the need can even evoke the discovery. The individual, in the lifetime where a skill was originally required, may have used it carelessly and so have decided to revisit it in circumstances that will ensure it full personal acknowledgement. Perhaps a life was cut short before self and others could fully benefit from a potent skill. It is by no means possible to see the complete picture – only to try to become more aware of the subtle web of interacting, evolutionary forces.

RENEWING SKILLS FROM OTHER LIFETIMES

How do we know, if it is not already abundantly clear, whether our 'karmic package' includes access to skills trained in previous lifetimes? For many, the gifts themselves begin to speak or even to compel. That unease with 'being normal' nags away at us until we decide to do something about it and/or seek help in so doing. For others it is maybe not the skill as such, which does the compelling, but an increasing sense of wanting a change of lifestyle. At such times, it is natural to make some kind of life review (similar to the one suggested in Exercise 1, page 22).

As we grow more confident in life, so we begin to rethink our values, questioning those of our parents and those of society. At the point of such a review we may decide that what we have is 'not so bad', and make a few changes to our priorities, but more or less settle for the status quo. The review helps us, perhaps, to appreciate life as it is, and to view it in a slightly or subtly different way. Yet we must also be prepared for the shock of viewing the rut or the groove in which we have got stuck. Some thoughts do not easily go away at such times: 'I have always been an adequate teacher, doctor, sales rep., shopkeeper, etc., but is this truly what I want from the rest of my life? Is there not something at which I excel? Something which makes my heart sing, in a way I have not so far experienced?'

We begin to realise that there is something within, demanding greater fulfilment. Perhaps we gave up a particular course, at school, in favour of another, considered to have more vital practical application. Perhaps some opportunities we craved were just not available, for a disparity of reasons.

As we make such realisations we may get that sinking feeling that we have left it too late. This is rarely so. *Whatever* the skill or gift, it is rarely too late to find some way of enjoying and expressing it. It may not be possible to become a professional ballet dancer or musician, but a seventy year old of my acquaintance discovered tap dancing and a sixty-year-old friend learned to play the saxophone well enough for his own and his family's pleasure.

A complete career change may or may not be 'on the cards'. Simply ventilating and allowing a modicum of expression to a previously repressed skill or gift can change your whole quality of life. Unavoidable commitments or a dreary daily routine that cannot easily be changed can become more bearable when life has been reorganised to allow time for study or practise of a skill which really resonates through our entire being.

'BEING' MORE COMPLETELY

Developing hidden or neglected talents and following the energy of change and fulfilment that leads to finding greater meaning in life, not only makes our hearts sing, but also puts us in touch with a greater wholeness of being. It is as though the present incarnate bead from the soul thread or grain from the core gains an unconscious but powerful sense of greater wholeness. A channel to what has gone before is opened positively and the present being becomes empowered.

Sometimes, maybe often, we are in circumstances that, with the best will in the world, refuse to be changed. What then, having found or glimpsed that which makes our heart sing, can we do? Knowing of karma can help us to accept frustrations, but a part of us will always long for freedom to express our true selves. Until change becomes possible it can help to alter our 'style' of doing things. If a repressed lover of beauty and harmony is, because of other commitments, obliged to work in a dreary office, accepting the challenge to make changes to beautify the workspace can give an outlet for frustration. Presenting work beautifully and refusing to identify with the limitations can lift spirits and even affect others around.

Although I now appreciate the experience I gained during my years of school teaching, I was never truly able to enjoy the work. When I realised that I am more essentially a healer than a teacher and found opportunities to focus on the pastoral opportunities that arose, I became happier in my self and, I believe, from that point onwards, a more efficient teacher. I am also convinced that channelling some of my frustrations in this way, set off the creative forces within me as well as the energies of synchronicity that eventually enabled me to change direction, even while having the ties and responsibilities of being a single parent.

Getting in tune with who you really are, at any age, helps you to find direction in life. The law of karma, in its wider application, provides an underlying fabric for constructive reflection on life. Allowing the theory of karma a place in our lives gives a basis for providing answers to those most pertinent of questions: 'Who am I?' and – 'What is my purpose in life?' The structures and tenets of belief, which must accompany any in-depth understanding of karma, help to put us in touch with our wider selves. We are not isolated beings, living out a chance existence, but emissaries for the evolution and perfecting of experience for our souls.

Case Study: Hilary

This case study illustrates a number of the points made in this chapter.

To all outward appearances Hilary was a 'high flier'. A very able pupil at school, she was channelled into studying sciences, mathematics and computer technology. Her father was also a mathematician and her mother a biologist. It seemed that Hilary was following in a family tradition. She obtained a good degree and found research work with a computer company. Quite quickly she moved into a highly paid position. She could afford a beautiful flat, lovely clothes and the world was her oyster. Despite this outward success, Hilary had few friends and, though she longed for a life partner, her relationships with men never lasted for very long. Because she felt there must be something radically wrong with her, in this inability to make relationships, she decided to go into therapy.

Obviously Hilary's mind had been highly trained. She had chosen a Jungian-oriented therapist who felt that there was a neglected or undiscovered intuitive and artistic side to Hilary. Coming from a family where science and the thinking function dominated and being pushed, as a 'high achiever', into sciences by her school, there were aspects of Hilary which had little opportunity to surface. From the world in which she worked and through family connections, the people Hilary met were basically of the same scientific, thinking type. Hilary felt there was something wrong with her when friendships did not deepen and relationships did not take off. She did not realise that she was basically looking for another dimension and that first of all she needed to release that dimension within herself. Although her outward success story at first sight belied it, Hilary was

really the traditional 'square peg in a round hole'. Her therapist recommended transpersonal workshops as an aid to
self-discovery.

In the workshops Hilary found herself to be totally at
home with imagery, symbolism, guided journeys and drawing
from her inner world. A completely new perspective opened
up for her and she longed for her weekends of inner discovery. Always good at her work, opening up and recognising her
intuitive side actually helped Hilary to be more innovative.
She made a natural change of 'style' in her work and felt more
fulfilled and whole as a result (see also page 118). In addition,
Hilary was meeting new people and experiencing a deep
connection with them. She felt socially at ease, as never
before, and, yes, there was a 'fairytale ending'. She met her life
partner at a workshop – a man in the process of change
himself. A former teacher, he had retrained as a journalist and
was becoming well respected in journalistic circles.

Yet, meeting her true love was not quite the end to
Hilary's journey of self-discovery and change. Through her
new-found friends she explored many new interests, one of
which was dance/movement. She had never danced before
and yet it was as though she had always danced. It became a
consuming passion for her. She was so naturally gifted that
she was readily accepted on to a professional training course
and later trained also to be a dance therapist. As she danced,
with the new ideas and contexts she was embracing, Hilary
became convinced that she had done it all before and that
her initial training had been as an Oriental temple dancer.

Exercise 8: Past Life Overview (1)*

This is a gentle, meditative exercise, safe for all, even if you

*For the second part of this overview see Exercise 9, page 137.

have not been familiar with or open to the concept of past lives before. Do not be disappointed if you don't get results the first time you try it – simply try again, on another occasion. Asking a friend or partner either to do it with you or to read the text for you can also be helpful. Do not take more than twenty minutes for this exercise. Set a 'pinger' as a reminder, if you are working alone.

Sit or lie in a comfortable but symmetrically balanced position. Make sure that you will be undisturbed, that you have a glass of water near you, a blanket for warmth, and crayons, pencils and paper on hand for any recording you wish to do.

Close your eyes and become aware of the rhythm of your breathing. 'Watch' your breath as it gradually slows down to a comfortable, natural, tempo. As you enter your inner being, find yourself on a beautiful sandy beach. The sea is calm, clear and gently lapping on to the smooth sand at the water's edge. The air is warm but fresh. There is sunlight on the water. Nearby there are some smooth rocks, which have been warmed by the sun. Go to these rocks and find a comfortable niche in them, so that you can sit with your back and head supported and look out to sea. Become even more fully aware of the play of the light on the tranquil waves.

Where the light meets the water, you can briefly see rainbow colours. Begin to focus on one of the colours of the rainbow, choosing it naturally or intuitively – or letting *it* choose you. Let the colour surround you, forming an egg shape around you, as you feel the safety of your rock beneath you. Absorb energy or healing from your colour.

Begin to think about the Earth and its history. Is/are there any place/s and historical time/s that particularly and positively attract you? From within the egg of your colour and the security of your rock, imagine that you are watching a film of that place and that time. Focus only on the good things or things you admire, that are associated with the place and time you are witnessing. Which aspects fascinate you? What sort of scene is your inner film showing you? Does the colour you have chosen want to move you on to more than one area of the globe or historical time? (Do not take more than ten minutes, in total, at this stage.) Simply watch and register what you have been drawn towards and then firmly bring yourself back to the rock, where you are lying, warmed by the sun, surrounded by an egg of energising, healing colour, looking out on a calm seascape.

Let the colour around you fade. Get up from your rock and walk along the beach, maybe barefoot at the water's edge, letting the waves gently wash over your feet. Gradually come back to the present, to the awareness of your body, in the present time. Feel the chair or the floor beneath you. Open your eyes and look around at your everyday surroundings. Drink some water. Take crayons, pencils, pens, paper and draw or record what you experienced during this meditation.

The intuitively chosen colour(s) in this meditation have a symbolic significance, though if they have a special, personal meaning for you, respect this above a general interpretation. Here is a list – though not an exhaustive one – of areas of experience or giftedness associated with the colours of the rainbow.

Red: Love of the earth, herbs, growing things; expertise with money; parenting; nurturing; pottery; love of animals; physical prowess.

Orange: Relationships; healing; nursing; surgery; creativity; government; leadership; passion; planning; travel.

Yellow: Leadership; drama/acting; military activities; vision; seership; magicianship; rulership; politics; knowledge; science; discovery; mathematics.

Green: Sensitivity; tenderness; healing; poetry; priest/priestess-hood; artistry; dance; interpretation; parenting; nurturing; service; contemplation; wisdom; wise counsel/judgement; beauty; harmony; channelling; religious orders.

Blue: Communication; writing; lecturing; acting/drama; the media; service; passion about causes/human rights/justice; singing; eloquence; interpretation; languages; channelling.

Indigo/Violet: Religion; service; rulership; philosophy; planning; channelling; ministering/pastoral work; spiritual leadership; inventing; healing; music; parenting; wisdom; heroism.

Chapter 7
ALL MY
RELATIONS

It knows not wrath nor pardon; utter-true
Its measures mete, its faultless balance weighs;
Times are as naught, tomorrow it will judge,
Or after many days ...

RECOGNISING LIFE'S TEACHERS • FORGIVENESS • THE BURDEN
OF EXPECTATION • UNFINISHED BUSINESS • LIVING MORE
CONSCIOUSLY THROUGH OUR RELATIONSHIPS •
EXERCISE 9 PAST LIFE OVERVIEW (2)

RECOGNISING LIFE'S TEACHERS

During the years of our formal education and learning most
of us will have met someone we could describe as a brilliant
teacher. Usually, such gifted individuals can inspire young
minds, give confidence and understanding and demonstrate
the true joys of learning. We sense their interest in each of
their pupils as individuals, feel cared for by them and will
willingly run that extra mile for and with them, in order not
to 'let them down'. Some of our life teachers have similar
qualities, whether within the family or in the wider area of
relationships. Learning is gentle, supported, inspired and
fun. We thus help each other to celebrate life's journey.

Karmically, we choose our family of incarnation to

provide the major setting and spur for our life's tasks. Our parents, siblings and relatives will be nurturers, teachers, providers of opportunity, healers and challengers. We may choose to be born surrounded by people and circumstances who will set us gently on our journey – or we may choose more difficult conditions. The process of incarnation, being present on Earth, and being born into our family of origin is immensely complex. Those who, on Earth, seem to be our harshest taskmasters, may be very close to us in our soul group. In the interests of learning our important lessons sooner rather than later, we may, before incarnation, have called on those closest to us, at a soul level, to play confrontational roles for us. It can take deep love to face the pain of being the catalyst for another's learning, if any degree of suffering is involved.

When we look back on life, often the troughs and the peaks come most easily to memory. The times when everything ticks along nicely tend to fade into relative insignificance. Things we can do or accomplish easily, we take for granted. Obstacles, challenges, frustrations and difficulties are demanding of the life skills we already have or are the means whereby we develop other life skills and maturity. Though there is no punishing authority forcing us to choose difficult incarnations, that higher, enduring part of ourselves – our higher selves – carrying our higher conscience can be a demanding taskmaster.

The whole spectrum of human relationships is a powerful arena for the working out of learning processes of all kinds. We all long for closeness, love and understanding. Loneliness and isolation are foreign to human nature and are recognised as two of the greatest trials a human can endure. In relating to others, we discover the best and worst about ourselves. Any inability in the field of human relationships is a potent trigger for self-searching. Difficulty in relationships is one of the most common reasons for bringing people into counselling. If we are without friends and 'significant others', we seek, and are motivated to, change. *Situations* in life may be of great moment in making us conscious. Our fellow humans, implicated in most life situations, will always be our greatest teachers. We may model ourselves on those who inspire us and whom we love, but those who oppose, criticise, reject or betray us are also great teachers. When we turn, from licking our wounds, to recognise this, karmic and evolutionary progress is often made.

Reflecting on the difficult people in our lives, and understanding the lessons we have learned from them, is difficult and often painful. We may carry the results of difficult encounters in our bodies, as symptoms. We frequently, and colloquially, use quite clear symbolic language to describe pains in the neck, back, shoulders, lumbar areas, upsets of the digestive system, nausea, coughs, breathing difficulties, even some 'accidental' injuries: 'She's a pain in the neck'; 'I wish he would get off my back'; 'I feel as though I am carrying the world on my shoulders'; 'It's as though I've been given a kick in the behind'; 'I can't digest all that is going on'; 'You make me sick!'; 'I'm coughing my heart out'; 'You suffocate me'; 'I'm only limping along at present (because of my sprained ankle)' – are but a few examples of this type of symbolism.

In recognising, as teachers, those who bring us difficult relationship experiences, and specifying the lessons they have taught, or are teaching us, we also help ourselves to overcome any victim consciousness we may have. Identifying with 'the victim' clouds our ability to take charge of our own lives and to see the opportunity that is a part of every crisis. In seeing the karmic and evolutionary laws positively, we can learn to take more conscious charge of our own destinies. We are not victims, but co-creators.

It is well known that a deeper understanding and rapprochement can result when people are willing to work at difficult relationships of all kinds. Couples working through marriage or partnership difficulties *do* come back from points of despair and imminent separation to find that 'the best is yet to come'. Families *can* get through periods of family rows and near rifts to realise a greater closeness. Creative compromises in relationships do happen – but more rarely if a sense of victimisation pervades. The response to an impassioned cry of 'I am nothing but your doormat', is often an equally impassioned 'But you are making me into a monster'! Only when we are willing to look at how such relationship dynamics have come into being and own our role in them, can we truly move on.

Resolution is not always possible. The wounds of betrayal, abandonment or rejection can be deep and disabling. Often it is right to walk away. Analysis, understanding, owning our hurt and our ability to hurt others, help to make sure that we do not walk on, or get left standing, with wounds that are too raw to heal.

In my practice I see a lot of people who are dealing with wounding caused by relationships. The first focus is always on the psychological understanding, healing and decision making that belong to the here and now. Working at this level will eventually include looking at what there is to learn from the situation itself and from the other people involved.

Considering these questions with people who are open to the wider dimensions of karma and spiritual evolution touches other levels. The work of self-healing, understanding and moving on has a deeper and more satisfying significance when things are put into a wider perspective and deeper reserves of emotional strength may be tapped. We may not fully understand or have intricate details of what has gone before, but knowing that the present difficulties have wider causes and do not stand in isolation, can help when it comes to being less hard on ourselves – and others. To be rejected or betrayed will always hurt, but to know that we are working on such things as karmic themes brings in that transpersonal and symbolic perspective, which nurtures survival and minimises scar tissue. Dealing with karmic issues can make experiences more intense. *Accepting* that something is bigger than the immediate and obvious gives the intensity its due proportion.

Our karmic teachers are those who move us deeply, either positively or negatively, and who leave deep impressions on us emotionally. Their presence in our lives may cause us to change direction, be jolted out of complacency, turn love into hate and cause whirlpools in previously calm waters. If it is essential that progress and consciousness should move forward on certain themes, then more than one intense teacher may appear until the issue is understood.

Case Study: Hannah

Sometimes, when we are in crisis, a subtle lifeline – or karmic plan – leads us to the right person at the right time.

Hannah's life was *in extremis* when she first met Beryl. She was unhappy in her marriage and exhausted with doing a job she disliked. She had no spiritual perspective, could not talk to her husband, had never got on well with her family of origin and was now finding life dreary and meaningless in the extreme. She was depressed and admitted to suicidal thoughts when at her lowest. Her young daughter was her only anchor to life itself and she hated having to leave Sarah with child-minders while she worked to help balance the family budget. Her husband did not help in the house and seemed blind when it came to any understanding of how difficult it was, physically and emotionally, for Hannah to juggle so many roles in life. He criticised instead of being supportive. He was jealous of the attention given by Hannah to her job and to Sarah. Though he loved Sarah in his own way, he was not a natural parent.

Beryl was a yoga teacher. Hannah had seen an advertisement for her classes and decided that she would give them a try. Beryl used a rainbow as a logo. Although Hannah already had so much to do she felt that she needed some colour and movement in her life and that yoga could be the answer.

Each yoga class began with thoughts on a spiritual theme and ended with relaxation and meditation. Beryl sensed the deep need in Hannah and encouraged her to stay behind for a few moments in order to give her personal encouragement and to suggest which yoga exercise she might concentrate on between lessons. Hannah borrowed some of Beryl's books and read them avidly.

In the course of time, Hannah realised that her relationship was not going anywhere. Leaving her husband, and taking Sarah with her, she found a small flat and a different job. She said she could never have taken such steps without Beryl's support. Beryl realised that she was becoming something of a mentor for Hannah, but worried about the intensity of her dependence. It seemed that this would have a natural resolution when Hannah was offered a good career opportunity, and better housing for herself and Sarah, if she moved to a completely different part of the country. She decided to take it and drew on Beryl for support as she arranged her move. At this point, Beryl felt that her work with Hannah had come to an end. She was able to recommend a teacher in the new area, gave Hannah a parting gift and made no promises to stay in touch.

Hannah had different expectations. When it became clear that Beryl was not willing to correspond or to be open to her becoming a personal friend, Hannah felt hurt and rejected. She accused Beryl of being responsible for all the changes she had made in her life and then abandoning her. A near breakdown threatened. Beryl recommended a therapist and slowly Hannah made insights about her own tendencies towards over-dependency and her fears about taking responsibility for herself. She began to see that spiritual growth was not all about meditation and interesting reading, but that it was also something to be put into practice in the mundane areas of life. She saw that Beryl was, indeed, a true teacher in every sense. She had not abandoned Hannah but had trusted her ability to walk her new path, make new friends, find new sources of support and thrive in her new life.

Hannah's dependence/independence theme did not end at this point. Throughout the years she attracted a series of life teachers towards her. She was continually challenged by her tendency to build up big expectations of others and to become too reliant on them. Inevitably the moment would come when these others found her too demanding, and so withdrew. Each time, Hannah revisited the same painful feelings of abandonment and rejection. She only saw clearly that one of her life's lessons was to learn independence, trust her own strengths and to receive support for herself by giving it to others, after a particularly painful, complex and dramatic re-play of the rejection/abandonment theme. As her eyes opened fully, she made a decision to become a yoga teacher herself and went on to become very successful in that field.

Not long after Hannah knew that she had accepted her

need to be truly herself, without complex reliance on others, she met a new partner, married him and now has a very happy relationship. This took her by surprise, since she had realised that she could be perfectly happy as a single woman. This can be the way with deep spiritual or karmic lessons – once we reach the point where neediness, for the wrong reasons, recedes, where the endurance test is no longer an endurance, the unexpected bonus comes.

FORGIVENESS

The concept of karma puts many spiritual issues into a wider context. Forgiveness is one of these. When we feel ourselves to have been wounded or betrayed by others within the span of this lifetime, the nagging hurt, rage, indignity and fear can complicate the process of reaching forgiveness. Yet most of us feel that forgiveness is important. The cry 'I wish I could forgive' is full of pain and self-recrimination. The all too familiar consequence of not being able to find it in our hearts to forgive others is that we reach a place where we cannot forgive ourselves. The devastation of the original betrayal is followed by a loss of self-worth in which the pain nags on. Release becomes complex.

Forgiveness is difficult to define. It is a process that goes beyond pardoning, excusing or compassion. When it is achieved, the one who forgives and the one who is forgiven enter into a dual 'state of grace'. A deep mutual understanding occurs. Hurts received and grudges borne are completely released.

Matters requiring forgiveness usually centre on betrayal of trust. Yet trust is an expectation, and sometimes we impose its burden on those who have neither asked us to do so nor are ready and able to carry it. Of course we need to nurture and nourish relationships that have trust at their core, but we can only trust each other, uncomplicatedly, when we have found deep trust in ourselves.

Acceptance has to be reached before forgiveness is achieved. This involves recognising, as we have already seen on page 124, that we are, inevitably, each other's teachers. Even betraying and being betrayed can be seen as lessons. When this insight is fully embraced, forgiveness becomes less of a problem. If the lesson had to be learned, then there is a need to thank, rather than to forgive, its teacher.

Putting forgiveness into the karmic perspective can open our eyes even more fully to the knowledge that, at the highest level, despite the difficulties we encounter in relationships of all kinds, there is nothing to forgive. Putting it into the wider continuum of previous existences relieves any sense of pressure. Our higher selves have chosen our obstacles for the present life as constructive challenges, in view of what has gone before. Accepting this enables us to come out on the other side of each one of them, with more strength, more creativity and more courage. With such acceptance, forgiveness has already, naturally, taken place. Opposition helps us to ask the right questions about our lives and thence to make decisions based on those questions. In this way we avoid unforgiving blame of others, and of ourselves. We can maintain self-regard and feel more in control of our choices.

THE BURDEN OF EXPECTATION

It is psychologically well recognised that in close relationships we seek ideals. Each of us has, deep within ourselves, an image of the ideal parent, friend, teacher, healer, guru, leader and partner/lover. Archetypal forces (see pages 20–1 and Glossary) drive us to seek these and bring them into our lives. When life is difficult, a common belief is that it would be less so, if only the perfect person/people to fit our needs would appear. Part of us clings to an underlying magical hope that this *will* happen – so much so, that when likely figures come along, we blindly project, or hook, our inner ideal on to them. This wish is so strong, that even when the first signs that our idol has feet of clay appear, we do not believe it. Even when it becomes abundantly clear that the one who is carrying all our expectations is less than we thought, part of us believes that it is all a bad dream or an illusion and that we shall wake up to find our idol restored. In this way, unconsciously, we set ourselves up for betrayal. Often, the idol who falls has done nothing other than pay us the compliment of being ordinary and human. Yet, when we are too close to our expectations, we cannot appreciate this. We become irrationally angry with such people, for not being who we set them up to be.

Frequently, our first experience of this is with our parents. Another psychological truth is that parents can only, at best, be 'good enough'. They have their own issues and hang-ups and can only do their best. Where parenting is reasonable, learning to see our parents as the ordinary, vulnerable humans they are is part of our growth process, aiding our own ability to venture into independent adult life. Where there are serious defects in the parenting we have received, we may need to let go of the belief that one day we shall wake up and find that our parents have changed overnight. Only on reaching this stage, do those who have suffered an emotionally deprived childhood, gain the strength to stop being 'inner orphans' looking for parenting from others, or from the state.

Hannah expected more than Beryl could, or was prepared to, give. She went on repeating this pattern, projecting expectations too big to be met, on to key figures in her life, until she learned that her true strength lay only in herself. We often say of young lovers that they are 'in love with love'. Throughout our lives, many relationships flounder when the nitty-gritty of everyday life barges in. Unless we can withdraw, or modify, our projections of perfection, life will continue to hold hard knocks for us. We need to remember that life in the raw contains smelly socks, dirty nappies, sleepless nights, morning moods and leaking roofs. Mature love sees the warts and loves them, too.

Hannah moved on in her life when she realised her own abilities and began to take joy in relying on herself. Transpersonal psychology (see Glossary) emphasises the need to find our inner strengths and resources, and to use archetypal patterns in a positive way as an aid to this. We can all gain access to our inner figures of wisdom, healing, nurturing, parenting and perfect partnership. When we do so, we are less likely to project these qualities outwards on to unsuspecting others. Relationships may become less dramatic or intense, in one sense, but they become more true and real in another. When we trust ourselves because we are in touch with our inner truth, we are far less vulnerable to being let down, failed, rejected or betrayed by others.

Wise, positive inner figures help us to relate to the archetypes of higher qualities (see page 29). Evolution and karma are linked to the development of this relationship. As we see our here-and-now, outer affinities more clearly, so we help ourselves to move on from retributive/repentant karma to the redemptive and transcendent stages (see page 56). Evolution, the benefits gained from experience in previous lifetimes resulting in an ability to draw on cumulative involvement with the archetypes, encourages our positive inner figures to become richer and more complete.

UNFINISHED BUSINESS

For each one of us certain life encounters will seem to be more highlighted than others, affecting us more powerfully or dramatically, whether positively or negatively. It is in meeting such people that we change our lives, make great insights, suffer, become inspired or undergo strong emotions, such as passionate love or hate. It is this very intensity that can signal to us that this is an important, and probably, karmic learning situation. These may be people we have met before, in a previous existence. (In the sense that though exactly the same personalities do not reincarnate, we instinctively recognise beads from the same thread or grains from the same core.) There may be unfinished business that our higher selves are resolute in bringing to our notice.

Many people worry about issues of 'unfinished business', whether it be psychologically or karmically. At both levels, if we try too hard we can add complexities to the original situation (see also Karmic enmeshment, page 90). Where there is a response from another person and we can work things through consciously, with recognition on both sides, then indeed old scores can be settled and hatchets laid to rest. Where there is no such response we can end up feeling very frustrated and disempowered, unless at some point we realise that we have done as much as we can. Ends may not be tied, corners may not be rounded, but sometimes we have to turn, or walk, away. If you have done all you can, but can go no further because there is no answering response from others involved, this does not necessarily mean that the business remains technically unfinished for *you*. The unresponsive party may have to meet a similar situation again, in this lifetime or another, but you need not be reinvolved, once clarity on the issue in hand has been gained.

LIVING MORE CONSCIOUSLY THROUGH OUR RELATIONSHIPS

To live more consciously through our relationships we need to develop the ability to observe ourselves dispassionately. The inner observer who is hyper-critical, over-judgemental, punishing or threatening is not truly helpful to our emotional and spiritual growth. The inner observer, who can stand slightly apart from every life situation and remind us to ask ourselves the right questions at the right time, is invaluable. Where relationships are concerned these questions need to include:

Am I seeing the whole person? Am I seeing the good points and minimising the aspects of this person I find difficult? Am I seeing only the bad points and minimising what this person has to offer? What do I want of this person? Am I sure that he/she has the resources to give me what I want? What price am I paying for what I want? Is it a price I can pay easily and willingly? Is there equality between us? Is there mutual give and take? If there is not equality, am I happy with the role I am playing/will play? Are there any seeds of jealousy here? Are we likely to play power games with each other? Is there mutual trust? How do my closest friends see this person? Am I seeking to be rescued? Am I being a rescuer? Is one side of our relationship so dominant as to make it difficult to see other facets? Does this person bring out wholeness, joy, humour and well-being in me?

Asking such questions is no guarantee that we will be able to answer them honestly. Even if we answer them, we may do so with limited vision. Things may still break down or erupt at a later point – but at least we sow the seeds for a greater consciousness about what is happening as it happens. If our souls are intent on certain encounters and lessons, they will usually happen, but where we ask questions and strive to observe what is happening, we are more prepared, learn more quickly and find more adequate solutions when crises strike.

Exercise 9: Past Life Overview (2)

Exercise 8 (on page 120) is designed to give you the opportunity to sense which parts of the world and historical times have been important for you in past lives. Exercise 9 gives more opportunity for you to see karmic situations and themes that have affected you in other lives. You may even begin to recognise characters from the past who are with you in a slightly different form in the present.

It is important that you use this meditation to let anything surface that is ready to do so. Do not have any particular situation in mind when you undertake it. Your psyche is wise (see Glossary). It will help you to see what you are ready to see. If you push for specific information, a meditative journey, such as this one, will be less successful.

It is best to do this exercise with a partner or in a small group. If you are undertaking it alone, set a pinger to ring not more than twenty minutes from the start. Read the whole meditation through several times before you begin and pay particular attention to the grounding instructions at the end.

Before you begin, take a piece of paper and write today's date – day, month, year – clearly on it. Put it where it will be easily visible and accessible at the end of this inner journey. Sit or lie in a comfortable but symmetrically balanced position. Make sure that you will be undisturbed, that you have a glass of water near you, a blanket for warmth, and crayons, pencils and paper on hand for any recording you wish to do.

Close your eyes and become aware of the rhythm of your breathing. 'Watch' your breath as it gradually slows down to a comfortable, natural tempo. Ask your higher self to watch over you during this journey and to lead you to whatever karmic information it is important for you to know at this time. As you enter your inner being, find yourself walking in a beautiful walled garden. The sun is shining warmly on the scene and the bricks of the wall are mellow. You are taking time to explore every part of the garden – enjoying the plants and the way in which the garden has been laid out and carefully tended. Curiously, you discover that there is a large mirror set in one of the garden walls. As you look into the mirror you realise that you are not looking at your here-and-now reflection, but are watching another self, from another time. As you continue to look into the mirror the story of this other self unfolds and you watch with interest. If at any time you find the story difficult to watch, know that you can simply turn away from the mirror and walk through other parts of the garden.

If you are happy to do so, you can continue to look into the mirror until the pinger, which you set to ring twenty minutes from the start of this inner journey, tells you that the time is up. When this happens, see the 'other you' fade. See only the reflection of your here-and-now self in the mirror. Turn from the mirror and walk through your favourite areas of the walled garden, feeling at peace. Sit for a while, on a bench or seat, in the sunshine.

When it feels natural to do so, begin to come back to the awareness of your body on the chair or floor, in your everyday surroundings. Feel the rhythm of your breathing. Open your eyes and look around you. Take a drink of water. Imagine that you are drawing a cloak of light with a hood right around you. Get up and walk around the room, being very conscious of your feet upon the floor. Sit down again and take the piece of paper on which you wrote today's date and write that date again, in another colour, then begin to draw or write those things from your journey, that you wish to remember.

Chapter 8
FINAL COMMENTS: LIFE'S JOURNEY

By this the slayer's knife did stab himself;
The unjust judge hath lost his own defender;
The false tongue dooms its lie; the creeping thief
And spoiler rob, to render.

WORKING WITH LIFE • THE EXTRA DIMENSION • LETTING
LIFE JOURNEY US • EXERCISE 10 WINDSURFER MEDITATION

WORKING WITH LIFE

The path of life is strewn with rocks, hazards, sharp corners and unsigned crossroads. The river of life has whirlpools, weedy areas, backwaters, rocks and undercurrents. On the sea of life we can become becalmed, storm-tossed, stranded on sandbanks or rocks, blown off course and caught in strong currents. The landscape of life contains bogs, volcanoes, deserts and thickets. On each of these symbolic life journeys, we are open to the elements. It is a wonder we continue to travel at all. Yet we do! Though at times we may become weary, fearful or disillusioned, individually and collectively we tend to cling to a belief in ourselves, our potential and the purposes of life. It is important to work with life, rather than against it.

Having a working model or hypothesis for the meaning of life gives us signposts for the journey and resources for coping with the hazards and obstacles. Many religious and spiritual models emphasise areas such as sin, punishment, the degradation of incarnation, being thrown out of paradise, shame for our natural drives and appetites and the need for us to be penitent from birth. Psychological models have aimed to make us more self-accepting, to normalise our natural instincts, to make us less shame-ridden, to free us from false authority hang-ups and to encourage us to find our true selves.

It is important to realise that the psychological and religious/spiritual fields are very different. Even transpersonal psychology, which brings in a spiritual perspective, is not, of itself, a spiritual or religious path (see Glossary). Religion can dampen creativity. Psychology, taken to certain extremes, can make us uncertain about our moral values and can seem to condone licentiousness of all kinds. Church leaders and psychologists have often been in conflict.

Yet the field of interface between different models or maps for the journey is important. 'Interface' is a term used to describe the area in which two different belief systems can meet and overlap. While recognising the power and language of each field in its own right, we can nevertheless find a meeting place between the two. That meeting place often means that we can enjoy the best of both worlds, personalise our own journey and strengthen our sense of meaning and purpose in life.

When our fears and doubts about ourselves and about anthropomorphic Gods sitting on thrones of judgement, calculating stiff punishments for us, are allowed to recede, the field of karma and reincarnation can give us valuable interface material. Karma is a spiritual law in its own right, yet also open to much wider interpretation. It does not have to be the law of a 'jealous God', but can be seen as a law of compassion, encouraging consciousness and enabling us to find and develop our highest, individual and collective potential.

Karma teaches us that we are often our own worst enemies. It encompasses retribution/repentance, but also offers us ways to become free of such burdens. We do not need to see obstacles as insurmountable, traps and cross-winds as totally destructive or to remain stuck in the bogs of life. These very obstacles can be our signposts or the challenges that enable us to develop our greatest strengths. An unsigned crossroads can either be seen as a place of impossible choice or as an opening to at least four different directions or opportunities. Our attitude to the path is important. The karmic law offers us numerous chances to change our attitude, to break the power of the pendulum swing between polarities and creatively to transcend all difficulties. We tend to hold on to the negative, as we find it more comfortable to control than to let go. If we can let go, life takes us, often more gently than we might imagine, and points the way naturally. Before we can let go, we have to learn trust. When we understand a law such as karma more fully as a law of wisdom, greater trust in life can develop.

THE EXTRA DIMENSION

Even within life, most of us are our own harshest critics or judges. Seeing our allotted time as some variant on the standard 'three score years and ten' gives us a certain time-scale as reference for 'how we are doing' with our lives. When we hit the 'decade' birthdays after twenty years old, we tend to ask ourselves 'What have I achieved?' We often consider this achievement in worldly terms or by expectations of our parents or the society we are living in. We consider it in terms of success in work, partnership, finance, family, sports prowess, achievement, the type of house we live in or the car we own. But life's pattern is given additional scope by the concept of reincarnation.

When certain milestones are passed, and we know that some things that we expected of ourselves or that others put out as expectations *of* us, are unlikely to manifest, we may grieve, feel a failure, lose impetus or grow old before our time. Reincarnation and the concept of many lifetimes can take our focus from the here and now, 'three score years and ten', into the greater, wider, longer concept of evolution and achievement through many lifetimes. Things we did not experience in this particular lifetime, we may have already accomplished in another. Things we have started and not finished or brought to full maturity can be taken up in another lifetime. Foundations we have laid will not necessarily be wasted. Another bead on our soul thread will use that basis and build on it.

Though karma and evolution, when seen with positive meaning, can help us to realise that there are no mistakes in life, it is still in our nature, whenever we review our lives, to deem ourselves failures in one area or another. As we get older we may spend energy on wishing that things had been different or that we could have put something right that we consider to have gone awry. Belief in reincarnation may help us to be able to live the final years of our lives more harmoniously and with less self-criticism. The final years are not the end of opportunity, but are leading towards a new beginning, a chance to make a new start from a new perspective, as well as to see our apparent 'failures' or omissions in a new light.

LETTING LIFE JOURNEY US

Yet we must not let go in the wrong way. It is always less painful when we can go with the flow, but we should not do so as a piece of flotsam or jetsam. Going with the flow means observing the currents and tides and using them to empower us. The surfer can ride the waves skilfully, but cannot make them happen – and, ultimately, is dependent on the pattern of the wave itself.

We cannot interfere with the basic and sacred design of the universe, but we can learn to use resources and energies proficiently and respectfully. What is true of our relationship to the greater universe is true of our personal, intimate and immediate universes. We are the microcosm within the macrocosm. Through personal management we learn wider management. Making the most of individual resources and pursuing self-knowledge without becoming narcissistic is the greatest contribution we can make to the whole.

At the psychological level we often pay a high price for that which we regard as security. We create our own worlds, but are infinitely more experienced at creating them destructively rather than constructively. It takes energy to hold on. When we let go, we may suffer a sense of loss. Yet, many losses can be followed by a sense of freedom and an upsurge of vitality.

'Let go and let God' is a well-worn and over-simplistic cliché, but there is an underlying truth within it, which we do well to contemplate from time to time. This can be particularly powerful when we let go, in the right way, not only to God, but to our higher selves, our higher wisdom and the karmic circumstances these parts of ourselves have chosen wisely for us. Letting go consciously is a far different prospect from having things wrenched out of our unwilling arms. Modern science has demonstrated that even chaos produces new and meaningful patterns. With the wonders of modern science to demonstrate that letting go leads to unforeseen beauty, our excuses for holding on lessen daily. The value of trust is being proven.

Case Study: Stuart

Stuart had a 'safe' job as an architect with a local authority. He was becoming increasingly frustrated by financial cuts and the resulting, extra, limiting rules and regulations governing his design work. He wanted to implement changes in his life. He felt himself to be addicted to security, yet irritated by it. He was an only child, born when his very conservative parents were in their forties, and he felt that he had never been a risk-taker and did not know how to become one.

Stuart was married to Marie, a midwife. They had met in their late thirties and basically had an excellent relationship. They had decided not to have children. Yet Marie, too, was feeling frustrated with her work where she also was becoming trapped and limited by increasing regulations and lack of permission to practise her skill as she wanted to practise it. Marie was pushing for adventure and change, while they were still young enough to enjoy it. Stuart felt that if he could not resolve his problem with security, his marriage might be at risk.

As we worked together Stuart began to see that he had chosen a very boundaried life. He had incarnated to his older, conventional, non risk-taking parents and had lived at home with them until they both died, within months of each other. He was artistic, but had chosen to channel that flair into the discipline of architecture. Stuart began to recognise that his karmic and evolutionary challenge was about moving from limitation and security to some degree of risk-taking. He recognised Marie as a dear life companion, but saw that she was becoming, particularly at this time, a powerfully challenging teacher for him.

In a series of images, Stuart first felt himself to be becalmed on the sea of life. He had a strong boat and had felt himself to be in non-threatening surroundings. He had been content to be becalmed. Now he felt the wind of change was coming, and despite the strength of his boat, he had forgotten how to sail. The wind was comparatively gentle and the waves it was bringing were not particularly dangerous to such a strong boat. I suggested that he need not raise his sails for the moment, but just check his boat and wait to see what the wind would bring. As his imagery developed, Stuart felt that unless he took some kind of charge of the direction of the boat, he was likely to be blown on to some rocks. Rather than risk this, he decided to row his boat to the safety of a sandy beach he could see. As he began to row, so the wind changed direction and gave him extra power for reaching the beach.

Stuart did not want either his own psyche or his marriage to founder on the rocks. He now knew that he must gather a combination of courage and trust, so that, together with Marie, some calculated life risks could be taken.

In fact the risks they chose together were momentous. They decided to emigrate to New Zealand, where career opportunities for both of them seemed very positive. He came to see me for a final time, just before their departure. He was confident and excited, prepared to take on whatever the new life had to offer. He felt that he was leaving past structures behind, but was glad to be free of the weight of them.

Exercise 10: Windsurfer Meditation

Sit or lie in a comfortable but symmetrically balanced position. Make sure that you will be undisturbed, that you have a blanket for warmth, and crayons, pencils and paper on hand for any recording you wish to do.

Become aware of the rhythm of your breathing. Follow each in-breath and out-breath, but let your breathing find its own, naturally quietened level without trying to control it in any way.

Enter your inner space or territory and find yourself on a beautiful sandy beach, warmed by the sun. Feel the texture of the sand beneath your feet. Watch the play of light on the water. Be aware of the rise and fall of the waves. Hear the sound of the waves and the seabirds. Smell the tang of the sea. Taste the saltiness of the sea on your lips.

There is a light wind blowing and you find yourself watching some windsurfers speeding over the waves. At this point you can continue to watch the surfers, or you can *become* one yourself. If you are watching, pick out one particular windsurfer to identify with. Watch, or directly enjoy, the way in which the surfer catches the wind, turns the sail, rides the waves, is ever aware of changes in the elements around.

The wind is a little changeable. Sometimes the surfers become almost becalmed and need to rely simply on riding the waves. In one area, the waves are bigger and there the surfers are obviously experiencing the peaks and the troughs. When the wind changes or dies down, they have to wait for wave power, high surf, before they can be more in control of their course.

These windsurfers are not totally at the mercy of the
elements, but their enjoyment and their sense of direction
is dependent upon their skilful interaction with wind and
waves. They are on the sea of life. Some ride skilfully, while
others sometimes lose the balance of their boards or their
sails. All recover, and set out again, enjoying the
challenges, the sense of speed and the perfecting of their
skills.

Watch, or surf, for a while longer. Get a sense of the power
of equilibrium. When you are ready to return to your usual,
everyday, outer world, bring this sense of power in
equilibrium with you.

Come back gently, in your own time. Keep a quiet space
around you in which to write or draw your experiences
during this meditation. Draw or write quietly and
meditatively too, making this a part of the exercise.

Finally, come back fully to your normal, everyday, outer
consciousness. Feel your feet firmly on the ground. Look
around you at familiar objects. Visualise a cloak of light
with a hood right around you, so that you take light with
you wherever you go, but are also protected by it.

> Such is the law which moves to righteousness,
> Which none at last can turn aside or stay;
> The heart of it is Love, the end of it
> Is Peace and Consummation sweet. Obey!

GLOSSARY

Archetypes/archetypal forces: By dictionary definition these are 'primordial images inherited by all'. Each human society is affected by forces such as peace, war, beauty, justice, wisdom, healing, death, birth, love, power – sometimes called the *archetypes of higher qualities*. The essence of these defies definition and we need images, myths, symbols and personifications to help us in understanding their depth and breadth. Tarot cards, which have ancient origins, have 22 personified or symbolised archetypes of the major arcana. These cover all aspects of human experience.

Aura/auric field: The energy field, which interpenetrates with, and radiates out beyond, the physical body. Clairvoyantly seen, the aura is full of light, colour and shade. The trained healer or seer sees or senses indications within the aura as to the spiritual, mental, physical and emotional state of the individual. Much of the auric colour and energy come from the chakras.

Chakras: The word 'chakrum' is Sanskrit and means 'wheel'. Properly speaking, chakrum is the singular form and chakra the plural but in the West it is usual to speak of one chakra and many chakras. Much of the colour and energy of the auric field is supplied by the chakras.
Clairvoyantly seen, they are wheels of light and colour interpenetrating with, affecting and affected by, the physical body. Chakras carry links to specific parts of the glandular system and might therefore be described as subtle glands. Most Eastern traditions describe a sevenfold major chakra system at the same time acknowledging varying large numbers of minor chakras. The names of the major chakras are: the Crown (at the crown of the head); the Brow (above and between the eyes); the Throat (at the centre of the neck); the Heart (in the centre of the body, on the same level as the physical heart); the Solar Plexus (just under the rib cage); the Sacral (two fingers below the navel); and the Root (in the perineum area). Working with the chakras aids physical, mental, emotional and spiritual health.

The seven major chakras carry the colours of the rainbow spectrum; red for the Root; orange for the Sacral; yellow for the Solar Plexus; green for the Heart; blue for the Throat; indigo for the Brow and violet for the Crown. This does not necessarily mean that the chakras *are* these colours, but that they are responsible for producing that colour note within the chakra team and the auric field. Any colour may be 'seen' or sensed in any chakra. It could be said that each chakra has its own full spectrum of colour. The presence, quality and degree of other colours reflects information about ourselves.

Psyche: Analytic and transpersonal psychologies have shown how complex the human personality is. The psyche refers to the total being, with all its drives, needs, conflicts, dis-ease, health, gifts and potential.

Self-actualisation: The transpersonal psychologist Maslow, spoke about self-actualisation. He felt that, when growth processes and necessary healing reached a certain point, every part of our being could find expression. The blueprint with which we come into incarnation could be actualised. Probably a totally self-actualised person has little need to remain longer in incarnation – and, being self-actualised, would finish the task in hand and die gracefully. However, there can be times in our lives when we feel that we are 'firing on all cylinders'. This can be cyclical, or part of the spiral of growth. Once attained it may fade again or become elusive for a while, but when we have touched it, even briefly, we know that we are capable of manifesting our full spiritual selves whilst in incarnation.

spiritual teacher or guide/Gildas/channelling: A spiritual teacher can be any mentor who helps us address the spiritual, philosophical aspects of living, being and existing and inspires our search for meaning. In this book when I refer to my spiritual teacher, I am speaking of Gildas, my discarnate guide. Such guides have been through many lifetimes or incarnations and are now working

from another dimension. By a slight shift of consciousness, I can be in touch with Gildas, feel his presence and mentally hear/register his words and teaching. I can then speak out or write down, what I am being told. This is a form of spiritual mediumship known as channelling. Increasing numbers of people today are discovering their ability to channel.

Tarot: is an ancient form of cards which can be 'read' for the purposes of divination. The 72 cards form a major and a minor arcana. The major arcana consists of 22 archetypes covering all aspects of human existence. The minor arcana has four suits, differently named in different sets of cards, but mostly representative of mind, body, emotions and spirit.

transpersonal psychology: This addresses the spiritual needs and aspirations of human beings as well as the behavioural. It concentrates on the importance of finding a meaning in life and of being creative and fulfilled in living, relating and making choices.

Yin and Yang: are Chinese words for the basic but opposite aspects of creation. Yin is receptive, feminine and dark. Yang is active, masculine and light. In the traditional yin/yang symbol one black and one white fish-like shapes nestle together to form a perfect circle. The eye of the black shape is white and the eye of the white shape is black, showing that the seed of each is contained in the other.

BIBLIOGRAPHY

Sir Edwin Arnold, *The Light of Asia*, Roberts Brothers, Boston, 1891

Edward Conze (trans.), *Buddhist Scriptures*, Penguin, 1959

Joan Grant, *Time Out of Mind*, Ayer Co. Publishers, 1940

Joan Grant, *Winged Pharaoh*, Ariel Press, 1999

Joan Grant, *Lord of the Horizon*, Ariel Press, 1998

Joan Grant, *Eyes of Horus*, Alliance Press, 1989

Joseph Head and S. L. Cranston, *Reincarnation*, Theosophical University Press, 1994

Raynor Johnson, *The Imprisoned Splendour*, Pilgrim Books, 1989

C. G. Jung, *The Archetypes and the Collective Unconscious*, R. F. C. Hull (trans.), Routledge, 1991

Rupert Sheldrake, *The Rebirth of Nature*, Park Street Press, 1994

Huston Smith, *The World's Religions*, Harper San Francisco, 1992

Ruth White, *Working with Guides and Angels*, Piatkus, 1996

Ruth White, *Chakras*, Piatkus, 1998

Ruth White, *Working with Your Chakras*, Piatkus, 1993

Ruth White, *Your Spiritual Journey*, Piatkus, 1998

INDEX

and Divine Essence 34
repentance 56–7, 58, 74
responsibility, personal 15, 86, 90, 91, 92, 130
retributive/repentant karma 33, 45, 52, 56–7, 59, 72, 73, 74–5, 87, 97, 98, 113, 114, 134, 142
rewards, karmic 113–14

Service, archetype of 28, 54
service 20, 51, 55, 59, 74, 103
soul, the 10, 26, 27, 35–6, 71, 76
    arrangement/structure of 34, 35, 46–7, 49
    and evolution 32
    evolution of 21–2, 27, 28, 34–5, 59, 76, 108, 114–15
    group 48
    and choice of incarnations 35, 41–2, 44, 45–7, 64
    and karmic choices 44, 45, 46, 48–9
    splitting of 76, 104
soul beads see beads, life/personality
soul families 49, 50, 51, 62, 74, 75, 77, 78
soul groups 49–50, 62, 74, 75, 77, 86
soul mates 50
soul memory 115
Source, Divine 27, 29, 34, 76, 103–4, 105
    union with 27, 36
spirit 26, 27, 32, 34, 35–6, 71
suffering 6, 16–17, 40, 74, 125

synchronicity 75, 87, 100–1, 118, 134

Tarot cards 28
Teacher, archetype of 30–1, 56
teachers 3, 44, 57, 98, 99–100, 113, 118
    karmic 63–4, 128
    life's 51, 68–9, 73, 124–8, 129–30, 132, 146
    spiritual 2, 102
therapy 42–3, 65, 119–20, 130
    see also counselling; transpersonal psychology
transpersonal psychology 3, 120, 134, 141
transcendent karma 56, 57–8, 87, 98, 134
true self, the 70, 72–3, 131, 141
trust 131–2, 134, 142, 145, 146
twin souls 62, 69, 75–7

unfinished business 135–6
Upanishads, the 11

Vedas, the 11
Victim consciousness 126–7

wholeness 3, 27, 47, 55–6, 117
Wholeness, archetype of 54
Work 98–9, 118

yin and yang 69–70, 76
yoga 129

Ruth White runs a number of courses, including courses in channelling, meditation, chakra work and spiritual growth. It is also possible to do a correspondence course in spiritual growth designed to individual needs.

For a programme of courses contact Ruth on 07808 610 386

(Correspondence will be forwarded via the publisher. Please write to Ruth White, c/o Piatkus Books, 5 Windmill Street, London W1P 1HF)